Microsoft®
Office 2007

VISUAL™
Quick Tips

Visual®

by Paul McFedries

BICENTENNIAL
1807
WILEY
2007
BICENTENNIAL

Wiley Publishing, Inc.

Microsoft® Office 2007 Visual™ Quick Tips

Published by
Wiley Publishing, Inc.
111 River Street
Hoboken, NJ 07030-5774

Published simultaneously in Canada

Copyright © 2007 by Wiley Publishing, Inc., Indianapolis, Indiana

Library of Congress Control Number: 2006936748

ISBN: 978-0-470-08972-9

Manufactured in the United States of America

10 9 8 7 6 5 4 3 2 1

1K/RS/RS/QW/IN

Trademark Acknowledgments

Contact Us

For general information on our other products and services contact our Customer Care Department within the U.S. at 800-762-2974, outside the U.S. at 317-572-3993, or fax 317-572-4002.

For technical support please visit www.wiley.com/techsupport.

MAY 17 2007

Wiley Publishing, Inc.

Sales

Contact Wiley at (800) 762-2974 or fax (317) 572-4002.

Praise for Visual Books

"I have to praise you and your company on the fine products you turn out. I have twelve Visual books in my house. They were instrumental in helping me pass a difficult computer course. Thank you for creating books that are easy to follow. Keep turning out those quality books."

Gordon Justin (Brielle, NJ)

"What fantastic teaching books you have produced! Congratulations to you and your staff. You deserve the Nobel prize in Education. Thanks for helping me understand computers."

Bruno Tonon (Melbourne, Australia)

"A Picture Is Worth A Thousand Words! If your learning method is by observing or hands-on training, this is the book for you!"

Lorri Pegan-Durastante (Wickliffe, OH)

"Over time, I have bought a number of your 'Read Less - Learn More' books. For me, they are THE way to learn anything easily. I learn easiest using your method of teaching."

José A. Mazón (Cuba, NY)

"You've got a fan for life!! Thanks so much!!"

Kevin P. Quinn (Oakland, CA)

"I have several books from the Visual series and have always found them to be valuable resources."

Stephen P. Miller (Ballston Spa, NY)

"I have several of your Visual books and they are the best I have ever used."

Stanley Clark (Crawfordville, FL)

"Like a lot of other people, I understand things best when I see them visually. Your books really make learning easy and life more fun."

John T. Frey (Cadillac, MI)

"I have quite a few of your Visual books and have been very pleased with all of them. I love the way the lessons are presented!"

Mary Jane Newman (Yorba Linda, CA)

"Thank you, thank you, thank you...for making it so easy for me to break into this high-tech world."

Gay O'Donnell (Calgary, Alberta, Canada)

"I write to extend my thanks and appreciation for your books. They are clear, easy to follow, and straight to the point. Keep up the good work! I bought several of your books and they are just right! No regrets! I will always buy your books because they are the best."

Seward Kollie (Dakar, Senegal)

"I would like to take this time to thank you and your company for producing great and easy-to-learn products. I bought two of your books from a local bookstore, and it was the best investment I've ever made! Thank you for thinking of us ordinary people."

Jeff Eastman (West Des Moines, IA)

"Compliments to the chef!! Your books are extraordinary! Or, simply put, extra-ordinary, meaning way above the rest! THANKYOU THANKYOU THANKYOU! I buy them for friends, family, and colleagues."

Christine J. Manfrin (Castle Rock, CO)

Credits

Project Editor
Sarah Hellert

Acquisitions Editor
Jody Lefevere

Product Development Supervisor
Courtney Allen

Copy Editor
Paula Lowell

Technical Editor
Jim Kelly

Editorial Manager
Robyn Siesky

Business Manager
Amy Knies

Editorial Assistant
Laura Sinise

Special Help
Barb Moore

Manufacturing
Allan Conley
Linda Cook
Paul Gilchrist
Jennifer Guynn

Book Design
Kathie Rickard

Production Coordinator
Adrienne Martinez

Layout
Elizabeth Brooks
Jennifer Mayberry
Melanee Prendergast
Heather Ryan

Screen Artist
Jill A. Proll

Cover Design
Mike Trent

Proofreader
Lisa Stiers

Quality Control
Melanie Hoffman

Indexer
Richard T. Evans

Vice President and Executive Group Publisher
Richard Swadley

Vice President and Publisher
Barry Pruett

Composition Director
Debbie Stailey

About the Author

Paul McFedries is the president of Logophilia Limited, a technical writing company. While now primarily a writer, Paul has worked as a programmer, consultant, and Web site developer. Paul has written nearly 50 books that have sold more than three million copies worldwide. These books include the Wiley titles *The Unofficial Guide to Microsoft Office 2007, Excel PivotTables and PivotCharts: Your visual blueprint for creating dynamic spreadsheets, Teach Yourself VISUALLY Windows Vista, Windows Vista: Top 100 Simplified Tips & Tricks, MySpace Visual Quick Tips,* and *Teach Yourself VISUALLY Computers, Fourth Edition.* Paul also runs Word Spy, a Web site dedicated to tracking new words and phrases (see www.wordspy.com).

How To Use This Book

Office 2007 Visual Quick Tips includes tasks that reveal cool secrets, teach timesaving tricks, and explain great tips guaranteed to make you more productive with Office 2007. The easy-to-use layout lets you work through all the tasks from beginning to end or jump in at random.

Who Is This Book For?

If you want to know the basics about Office 2007, or if you want to learn shortcuts, tricks, and tips that let you work smarter and faster, this book is for you. And because you learn more easily when someone *shows* you how, this is the book for you.

Conventions Used In This Book

❶ Introduction
The introduction is designed to get you up to speed on the topic at hand.

❷ Steps
This book uses step-by-step instructions to guide you easily through each task. Numbered callouts on every screen shot show you exactly how to perform each task, step by step.

❸ Tips
Practical tips provide insights to save you time and trouble, caution you about hazards to avoid, and reveal how to do things with Office 2007 that you never thought possible!

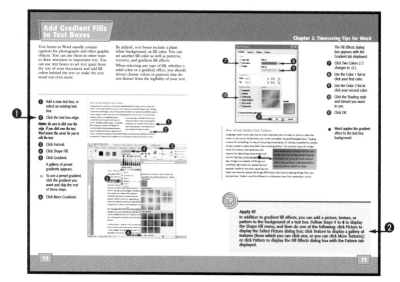

In order to get this information to you in a timely manner, this book was based on a pre-release version of Microsoft Office 2007. There may be some minor changes between the screenshots in this book and what you see on your desktop. As always, Microsoft has the final word on how programs look and function; if you have any questions or see any discrepancies, consult the online help for further information about the software.

Table of Contents

chapter 3 — Increase the Power of Your Spreadsheet with Excel

chapter 4 **Enhance Your PowerPoint Presentations**

chapter **5** **Customize and Optimize Outlook**

chapter **6** **Improve Your Database Productivity Using Access**

Chapter

1

Lighten Your Workload with General Office Techniques

Are you looking for ways to speed up your work with the programs in Microsoft Office? This chapter shows you some techniques for customizing programs and for working smarter and faster in the Office applications.

Literally dozens of techniques exist that you can apply to speed up your work in the Office programs. For example, did you know that you can right-click over screen elements to display a shortcut menu of related commands? If you right-click over text in Word, the shortcut menu lists commands such as Cut, Copy, and Paste. The menu also allows you to access the Font dialog box where you can change the formatting of your text. You can also find commands on the shortcut menu to help you improve your writing skills, such as the Lookup command, which opens Word's

Thesaurus where you can look up related synonyms. You can also use the right-click feature in the other Office programs to quickly access a relevant shortcut menu.

Keyboard shortcut keys, which activate common commands and features when you press a few keys, are another overlooked way to speed up your work. The trick to utilizing these shortcuts is to memorize the keyboard selections for the commands you use the most. With a little practice, memorizing keyboard shortcuts becomes second nature.

You can use the techniques in this chapter to customize your Office programs, files, and graphics you use across the Office programs. Customizing the Office programs can really increase your productivity.

Quick Tips

Shorten the AutoRecover Interval

You can minimize the chance that a system crash will destroy unsaved work by using a shorter AutoRecover interval.

A power failure, lightning strike, program hang, or Windows crash can occur at any time, and the result is often the inadvertent and sudden shutdown of the program and whatever document or documents you were working on. If you have not saved your work for a while, you will lose some or all of those changes.

Besides saving frequently, you can minimize the amount of work lost if your document shuts down without warning by shortening the AutoRecover interval. AutoRecover periodically tracks changes made to a document, and in the event of a program crash enables you to recover files that had unsaved changes.

① Click Office.

② Click *Program* Options (for example, Word Options).

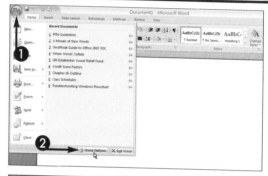

The Options dialog box appears.

③ Click Save.

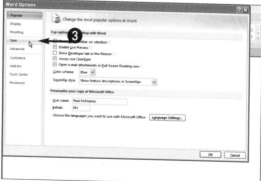

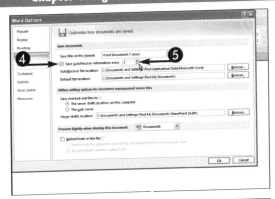

④ Click Save AutoRecover Information Every (☐ changes to ☑).

⑤ Click the spin buttons to set the frequency with which the program saves the AutoRecover data.

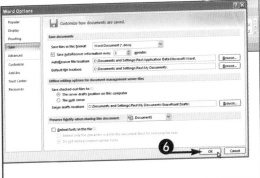

⑥ Click OK.

TIP

Caution!
For small documents, the shorter the AutoRecover interval the better. However, for large documents, saving the AutoRecover data can take the program a noticeable amount of time, so a very short interval can slow you down. Try a 4- or 5-minute interval as a compromise. If you are using an extremely large Excel workbook, you can turn off AutoRecover. In Excel, follow Steps **1** to **3**, click Disable AutoRecover for This Workbook Only (☐ changes to ☑), and click OK.

Learn Shortcut Keys Faster

You can use keyboard shortcut keys to greatly speed up your work in an Office program. Shortcut keys allow you to quickly activate a command instead of using a mouse.

The Office toolbars also allow you to quickly activate commands and features with a click of the mouse, but if you need to access a command while you type in data, you may not want to stop typing to switch to the mouse to click a toolbar button.

You can tell an Office program to list keyboard shortcut keys along with Ribbon button names and descriptions. (Note that this option is not available in Excel.)

① Click Office.

② Click *Program* Options (for example, Word Options).

The Options dialog box appears.

③ Click Advanced.

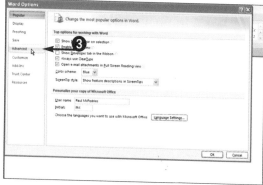

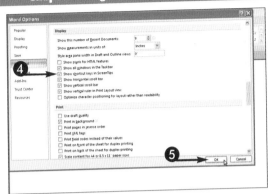

④ Click Show Shortcut Keys in ScreenTips
(☐ changes to ☑).

⑤ Click OK.

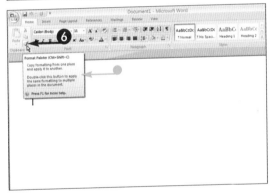

⑥ Move the mouse pointer over a Ribbon button.

● A ScreenTip box appears detailing the button name along with the equivalent shortcut key combination for activating the command.

Did You Know?

The Office 2007 programs display enhanced ScreenTips that include not only the name and shortcut key (if any) of each Ribbon feature, but also a short description of each feature. To control the ScreenTips' appearance, follow Steps **1** and **2**, click Popular, and then click an option in the ScreenTip Style list: Show Feature Descriptions in ScreenTips, Don't Show Feature Descriptions in ScreenTips, or Don't Show ScreenTips.

Customize the Quick Access Toolbar

You can put the commands that you use most often just a mouse click away by adding them to the Quick Access toolbar.

The Office 2007 Ribbon interface takes a bit of getting used to because it is such a radical departure from the traditional menu-and-toolbar interface. However, once you become accustomed to the layout of the tabs and groups, and once you see the power of the galleries and

lists, you will wonder how you did without the Ribbon.

As efficient as the Ribbon interface is, you may find that you have certain commands that you use constantly, and the several clicks required by the Ribbon are inefficient. You can fix this problem by adding common commands to the Quick Access toolbar for one-click operation.

---

1 Click Customize Quick Access Toolbar.

● If you see the command you want to add, click the command and skip the rest of these steps.

2 Click More Commands.

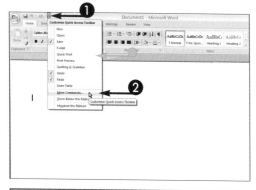

The Options dialog box appears with the Customize page displayed.

3 Use the Choose Commands From drop-down list to click the category of command you want to add.

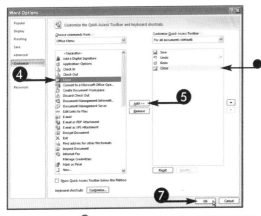

④ Click the command you want to add.

⑤ Click Add.

● The program adds the command to the list of items on the Quick Access toolbar.

⑥ Repeat Steps **3** to **5** to add more commands to the Quick Access toolbar.

⑦ Click OK.

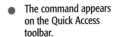

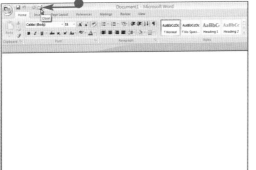

● The command appears on the Quick Access toolbar.

Note: *To remove a command from the Quick Access toolbar, right-click the command and then click Remove from Quick Access Toolbar.*

More Options!
By default, the Quick Access toolbar appears above the Ribbon, to the right of the Office button. This position limits the size of the Quick Access toolbar because of the program's title bar. If you want to get more commands on the Quick Access toolbar, move it below the Ribbon. Click Customize Quick Access Toolbar and then click Show Below the Ribbon.

Embed TrueType Fonts While Saving

You can ensure that other people who read your document see it with the proper font formatting by embedding your fonts in the document.

If you use some unusual TrueType fonts in a Word document or PowerPoint presentation that you plan on sharing with other people, your formatting efforts will be wasted if the other users do not have those fonts installed. To solve this problem, save your work with the

TrueType fonts embedded in the document, which ensures that the other users will see your document exactly as you designed it.

Word and PowerPoint enable you to embed either just the characters you used in the document, which reduces the file size, or every possible character in the font, which enables the other users to add new characters in the font.

① Click Office.

② Click *Program* Options (for example, Word Options).

The Options dialog box appears.

③ Click Save.

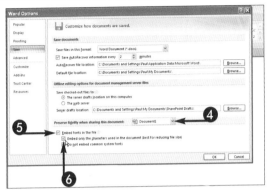

④ Use the Preserve Fidelity When Sharing This Document list to click the document in which you want to embed the fonts.

⑤ Click Embed Fonts in the File (☐ changes to ☑).

⑥ Click here to embed just the characters you used in the document (☐ changes to ☑).

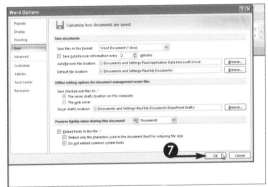

⑦ Click OK.

TIP

More Options!

In the Save page of the Options dialog box, the Do Not Embed Common System Fonts check box is activated by default. This makes sense because the other user's computer should have the same system fonts. If you know that this is not the case, deactivate this check box to embed the system fonts, as well.

Preview a Document Before Opening It

You can make launching a document more efficient by looking at a preview of the document before you open it.

If you have a large number of documents in a folder, remembering which file contains the information you are looking for can be difficult. Giving documents descriptive filenames can help, but you still may have times when you are not sure what is in a file.

You could simply open the document to see what it contains, but you could easily end up wasting quite a bit of time trying to find the document you want. To avoid this problem, you can instead display a preview of a selected document in the Open dialog box.

① Click Office.

② Click Open.

Note: You can also choose the Open command by pressing Ctrl+O.

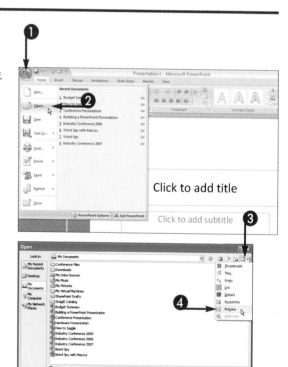

The Open dialog box appears.

③ Click the Views drop-down list.

④ Click Preview.

- The Preview pane appears.

5 Click the file you want to preview.

- The first part of the file appears in the Preview pane.

6 Repeat Step **5** until you find the file you want to open.

7 Click Open.

The program opens the file.

More Options!

If you are working with PowerPoint documents, the Preview pane shows you the first slide in the presentation. Another way to preview the first slide in any PowerPoint document is to switch to the Thumbnails view. A thumbnail is a preview that replaces (in this case) the normal PowerPoint file icon. To switch to this view, follow Steps **1** to **3**, and then click Thumbnails in the Views list.

Customize the Places Bar

You can make navigating folders in the Open and Save As dialog boxes easier by adding your favorite folders to the Places bar.

The left side of the Save As and Open dialog boxes includes icons for several common locations: Trusted Templates, My Recent Documents, Desktop, My Documents, My Computer, and My Network Places. The area that contains these icons is called the Places bar.

If you have two or more folders that you use regularly (for example, you might have several folders for various projects that you have on the go), switching between them can be a hassle. To make this chore easier, you can customize the Places bar to include icons for each of these folders. That way, no matter which location you have displayed in the Save As or Open dialog box, you can switch to one of these regular folders with a single click of the mouse.

---

① Click Office.

② Click Open.

Note: *If you prefer to use the Save As dialog box, click Save As, instead.*

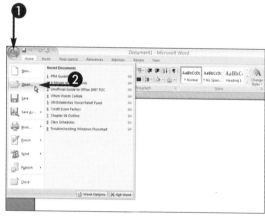

The Open dialog box appears.

③ Open the folder that you want to add to the Places bar.

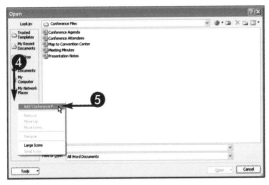

④ Right-click an empty section of the Places bar.

⑤ Click Add *Folder*, where *Folder* is the name of the open folder.

● Office adds an icon for the folder to the Places bar.

⑥ Click Cancel.

You can now navigate to the folder by clicking its icon in the Places bar.

More Options!
To manage a folder icon you have added to the Places bar, right-click the folder icon and then click one of the following commands: Click Move Up to move the folder icon higher; click Move Down to move the folder icon lower; click Rename to rename the folder icon; and click Remove to delete the folder icon from the Places bar.

Manage Computer Files from Any Office Program

You can manage your computer files from within any Office program.

For example, you may want to save a new Word file to a new folder in the My Documents folder (or the Documents folder, in Windows Vista). You can create the new folder in the Save As dialog box and then save the file to the new folder.

You can also edit folder names, delete folders and files, and move files to other folders. In addition, you can view the contents of your computer hard drive or other disk drives and conduct a search for a specific file. You can perform the same procedures in the Open dialog box.

CREATE A NEW FOLDER

① Click Office.

② Click Open.

You can also press Ctrl+O.

Note: Outlook includes different features for managing files and messages. See your Outlook documentation for more information.

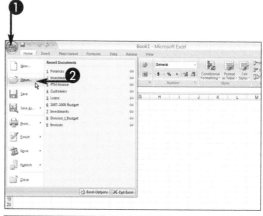

The Open dialog box appears.

③ Click the Create a New Folder button.

You can also press Alt+4.

The New Folder dialog box appears.

④ Type a new folder name.

⑤ Click OK.

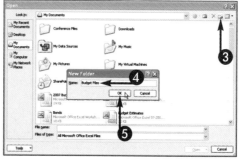

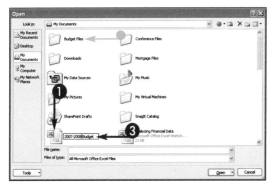

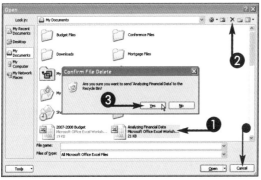

● The program adds the new folder.

RENAME A FILE

① Click the file you want to rename.

② Press F2.

A text box appears around the filename.

③ Type the new filename.

④ Press Enter.

The file is re-named.

DELETE A FILE

① Click the file you want to delete.

② Click the Delete button.

You can also press the Delete key on the keyboard.

A confirmation prompt window appears.

③ Click Yes.

Office deletes the file.

● You can click Cancel to exit the Open dialog box without opening a file.

TIP

Did You Know?

You can use shortcut menus within the Open and Save As dialog boxes. For example, right-clicking a filename activates a shortcut menu that lists related commands, such as Open and Print. Clicking the Print command prints the file without opening the program window.

Store Files in a Different Default Location

You can tell Office where to store the files that you create. When you open the Save As dialog box to save a file in Word, Excel, PowerPoint, and Access, these programs select the My Documents folder as the default working folder.

Rather than manually selecting a different folder from the My Documents folder

each time you save, you can tell Office to save your files to a default folder of your choosing.

This feature is handy if you use a different folder to store most of your documents. For example, you might be using a second hard drive that has more space, or you might be using a network folder.

① Click Office.

② Click *Program* Options (for example, Word Options).

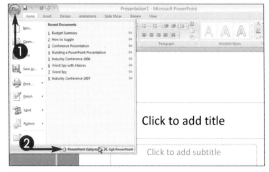

The Options dialog box appears.

③ Click Save.

If you are using Access, click Personalize, instead.

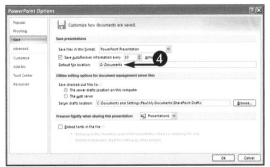

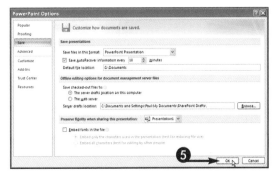

④ Inside the Default File Location field, select the text and type the desired name of the folder.

In this example, the new folder is named Documents and it resides on drive G.

In Access, click inside the Default Database Folder field to select the text, and then type a folder name.

⑤ Click OK.

Office assigns the new default folder.

Customize It!

Rather than specifying a different default folder in Office, you can move the My Documents folder (or Documents, in Vista) to a new location. For example, if you have a second hard drive that is faster or has more free space, you can move My Documents (or Documents) to that drive. Click Start, right-click My Documents (or Documents), and then click Properties. In the Target tab (the Location tab, in Vista), click Move to open the Select a Destination dialog box. Click the drive or folder you want to use, and then click OK.

You can inspect your documents to ensure that they do not contain any data that would compromise your privacy.

Office documents may contain data that can unwittingly disclose information about you, other people who have used the document, file locations, e-mail addresses, and much more. This type of information is known as *metadata* and

you should take steps to minimize or remove metadata.

To help you eliminate metadata and other private content, Office 2007 offers the Document Inspector, which you can use to automate the removal of the document data such as reviewer comments and annotations, document properties, headers and footers, hidden text, and text formatted as invisible.

① Open the document you want to inspect.

② Click Office.

③ Click Prepare.

④ Click Inspect Document.

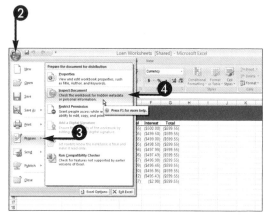

If the document has unsaved changes, the program asks whether you want to save the document.

⑤ Click Yes.

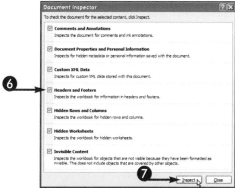

The Document Inspector appears.

6 Click the check box for any document content you do not want inspected (☑ changes to ☐).

7 Click Inspect.

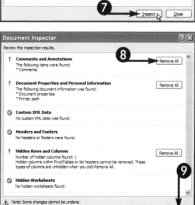

The Document Inspector checks the document and then displays the results.

8 To remove private information, click Remove All wherever it appears.

9 Click Close.

Did You Know?

You can assign a password to make your files private. In Word, Excel, and PowerPoint, click Office, Save As to open the Save As dialog box. Click Tools, General Options, and then type a password to open the file and a password to modify the file. Click OK. In Access, click Office, Open. Click the database, and then click Open, Open Exclusive. Then click Database Tools, Encrypt with Password.

Save a Document as an XPS File

You can save an Office document as an XPS file that people without Office can view.

What do you do if you need to share information with people who do not have Office? You could save the document as a Web page, but the page may not look the same as the original, and other users can easily copy the information and republish it. You could also publish the document

as a PDF file, which will look just like the original, and you can prevent copying, but PDF software is expensive.

A better solution is to use Microsoft's new document format called the XML Paper Specification, or XPS. It will look just like the original, you can control the content, and you can use Word, Excel, or PowerPoint to create the XPS file free.

---

① Open the document you want to save as an XPS file.

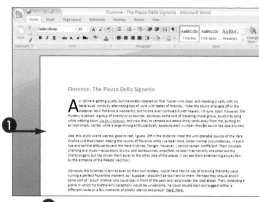

② Click Office.

③ Click the arrow beside the Save As command.

④ Click PDF or XPS.

Note: If you do not see the PDF or XPS command, you need to install the Save As PDF or XPS add-in. Go to www.microsoft.com/downloads and search for XPS.

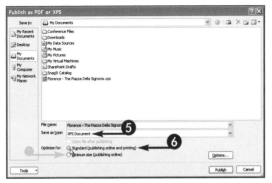

The Publish as PDF or XPS dialog box appears.

⑤ In the Save as type list, click XPS Document.

⑥ Click Standard if you intend to distribute the XPS document online or you want to print the XPS document (○ changes to ◉).

● Click Minimum Size, instead, if you only want to distribute the XPS document online.

⑦ Click Publish.

The Office program saves a copy of the document in the XPS format.

Did You Know?

For the XPS format to be useful, other people need to have an XPS viewer program. Fortunately, XPS uses XML (eXtendable Markup Language) for the document syntax and ZIP for the document container file, so it is based on open and available technologies. Microsoft is licensing XPS royalty-free, so developers can incorporate XPS viewing and publishing features into their products without cost. Also, support for XPS is built into Windows Vista, so all Vista users can view XPS files.

Turn Scanned Documents into Text

You can use the Optical Character Recognition, or OCR, capabilities in Office to convert a scanned document into text. You can then import this text into Word and edit it.

If you have a scanner hooked up to your computer, you can activate the Office Document Scanning program and convert the document into a Tagged Image File Format (TIFF) file, which is a common graphics file format. You can view the file in the Office Document Imaging program and export it to Word as a document file.

The Document Scanning program offers you several presets for scanning your document.

① Click Start.

② Click All Programs.

③ Click Microsoft Office.

④ Click Microsoft Office Tools.

⑤ Click Microsoft Office Document Scanning.

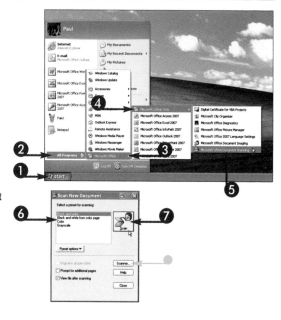

The Scan New Document dialog box appears.

⑥ Click a preset option.

The default, Black and White, works best for scanning text.

You can click the Color preset for artwork.

● If you need to specify a scanner, click Scanner and choose a scanner.

⑦ Click Scan.

The Office Document Scanner scans the page.

8 Click Close.

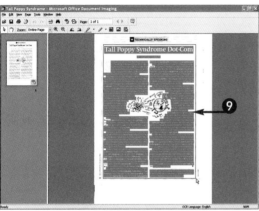

The scanned TIFF image of the document appears in the Office Document Imaging window.

9 If you only want to convert part of the document, click and drag the mouse over the text you want to use.

More Options!
If you receive an error when scanning, return to the Scan New Document dialog box and click Scanner. In the Choose Scanner dialog box, click Use Automatic Document Feeder (☐ changes to ☑), click Show Scanner Driver Dialog Before Scanning (☐ changes to ☑), and click OK.

continued

You can export scanned text from the Document Imaging program into other Office programs. Optical Character Recognition (OCR), also called *text recognition*, is software that analyzes a scanned page and attempts to convert it into editable text characters.

If you want to export the scanned document text into another Office application besides Word, you can copy the text from the Document Imaging window and paste it into another file.

Once you convert a scanned document into text, you can use the Document Imaging program window to search for text within the document, annotate the document, fill out form fields, and more.

⑩ Click Tools.

⑪ Click Send Text To Word.

The Send Text To Word dialog box appears.

⑫ To convert just the selected text, click Current Selection (○ changes to ◉).

● If you want to convert all the text, click All Pages, instead (○ changes to ◉).

⑬ If you prefer not to include any images from the original document, click Maintain Pictures in Output (☑ changes to ☐).

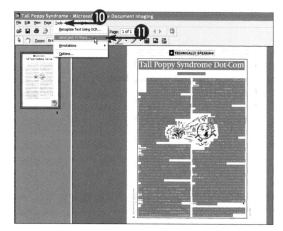

⑭ Click OK.

Word opens and displays the scanned document as text.

You can now edit the text as needed.

The Office Document Imaging window remains open onscreen until you close it.

Did You Know?

With the Document Imaging program, you can convert e-mail attachments and faxes into editable documents. For example, you may exchange important faxed documents with a mortgage company. Using the OCR capabilities in the Document Imaging program, you can convert these faxes from TIFFs into editable data. For images, click File and then Open; for other document types, click File and then Import.

Diagnose Office Problems

You can use the Office Diagnostics program to run a series of tests to help determine why a computer is crashing.

If you are having trouble with your system crashing, Office comes with an Office Diagnostics utility that can help you pinpoint the problem. Office Diagnostics runs a series of tests on different parts of your system. Some of

these steps focus on Office itself. For example, Office Diagnostics checks for corrupted Office files or Registry settings, available Office updates not yet installed, or solutions to known Office problems. More generally, Office Diagnostics also runs tests on your system's memory and hard disk. If any problems are found, the program offers solutions that you can try.

---

① Click Start.

② Click All Programs.

③ Click Microsoft Office.

④ Click Microsoft Office Tools.

⑤ Click Microsoft Office Diagnostics.

The Microsoft Office Diagnostics window appears.

⑥ Click Continue.

The Start Diagnostics window appears.

7 Click Start Diagnostics.

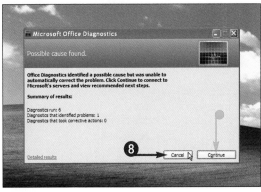

Office Diagnostics runs the tests on your system and then displays the results.

8 If Office Diagnostics did not find any problems, click Cancel.

● If problems were found, click Continue to display an Office Online Web page that explains the results and offers suggested solutions.

Did You Know?

If your computer is crashing frequently, you could lose unsaved work. To help prevent this situation, be sure to reduce the time your programs take between AutoRecover background saves, as described in the "Shorten the AutoRecover Interval" task earlier in this chapter. If after a crash you cannot open a document, click Office and then click Open to display the Open dialog box. Click the document, click the Open button's menu, and then click Open and Repair.

Customize Clip Art with the Ungroup Command

You can customize clip art and other illustrations you insert into your Word, Excel, or PowerPoint files using the Ungroup command.

To edit a picture, you must first convert the image into an Office drawing object. You can then use the Drawing Tools to ungroup the picture, which enables you to select a specific part of the picture to modify. For example, you can edit a picture element by changing the color or size, or you can delete an element. When you finish editing the picture, you can apply the Regroup command to reassemble the separate components into one picture again.

① Click the clip art you want to edit.

② Click Format.

③ Click Group.

④ Click Ungroup.

All the parts of the object are selected by default.

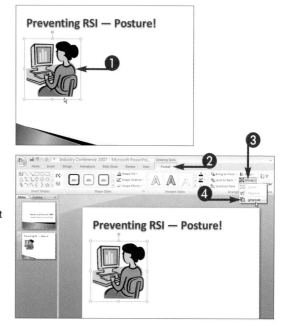

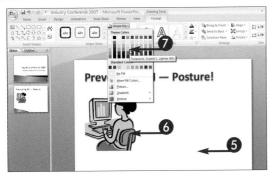

5 Click outside the object to deselect the elements.

6 Click a part of the object you want to work with.

7 Modify the part. For example, to change its color, click Shape Fill and then click a color.

In this example, the color of the woman's top was changed.

To delete an element, click it and then press Delete.

8 Repeat Steps **6** and **7** to continue editing parts of the object as needed.

9 Click Format.

10 Click Group.

11 Click Regroup.

Office regroups the image again as one object.

TIP

Customize It!
You can remove the colored background of a picture or bitmap image. Click the image, click Format, click Recolor, and then click Set Transparent Color. Click the background to make it transparent. For best results, change the background color of the document. This technique does not work on regular clip art images.

Position Clip Art Using Text Boxes

You can use text boxes to position clip art and other graphics in a document. Text boxes are ordinarily used as containers for text that you want to set apart from the regular document text.

Placing graphics in a document without text boxes is not always an easy procedure.

But by placing your clip art in a text box, you have greater control over the position and size of the graphic on the page.

You can also apply the options found on the Format tab to change the box fill color or add a border. By default, text boxes include a border.

1 Click Insert.

2 Click Text Box.

3 Click Draw Text Box.

4 Click and drag where you want the text box to appear.

● A text box appears.

5 Click Insert.

6 Click Clip Art.

● The Clip Art task pane appears.

7 Click the art you want to use.

● The clip art appears in the text box.

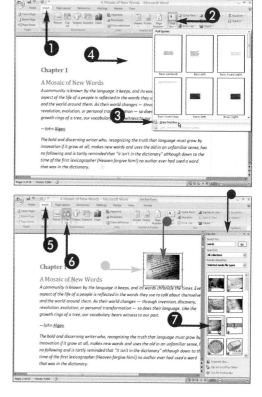

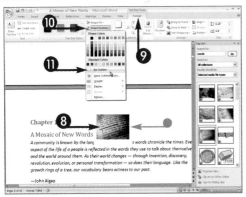

8 Click and drag the text box and drop it in the position you prefer.

The text box appears in the new location.

9 Click Format.

10 Click Shape Outline.

11 Click No Outline.

● The text box border disappears.

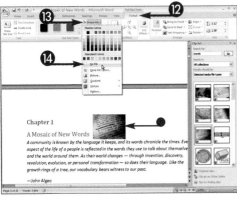

12 Click Format.

13 Click Shape Fill.

14 Click No Fill.

● The text box background becomes transparent, enabling you to see the document text covered by the box.

Customize It!

To change the size of the clip art, you do not need to change the size of the text box. Instead, click the clip art to select it. Office displays selection handles on the corner and sides of the image. Click and drag a selection handle until the image is the size and shape you want. When you release the mouse button, Office resizes the text box automatically to accommodate the new size of the clip art.

Timesaving Tips for Word

Microsoft Word is the workhorse of the Office suite. Not only can you use Word to produce all kinds of written communication, but also to easily integrate data from other Office programs. You can bring in Excel data, PowerPoint slides, and Access tables to create dynamic reports, research papers, letters, newsletters, and more.

Word offers an impressive abundance of commands and features. Each new version brings more features and techniques for improving and building your documents. In Word 2007, for example, you can write and post entries to your blog directly from Word. You can quickly access these features through shortcuts, tricks, and tips that make your use of Word more productive and speedy.

A great way to make Word work more effectively for you is to customize the basic program features; for example, you can revise the toolbars to include the buttons you use frequently. You can use the Word Options dialog box to turn on features you use the most and turn off features you rarely need. For example, you may want to control the number of items that appear on Word's Recent Documents list.

In addition to acclimating yourself to Word program options, you can also take advantage of the Word features that enable you to navigate long documents, such as a table of contents and bookmarks.

Quick Tips

Utilize Status Bar Shortcuts

You can use the status bar to quickly access several useful features to speed up your work.

Word divides the status bar into several sections that display data such as the current section, page, line, and column, the document word count, and the document's current spelling and grammar check status.

Word 2007's status bar is much more customizable than the one in previous versions. Word 2007 comes with a Status Bar Configuration menu that enables you to toggle more than 20 different status items on and off. Even if you do not turn on an item, in many cases you can display the Status Bar Configuration menu to see the item's current value.

TOGGLE STATUS BAR FEATURES

1 Right-click the status bar.

● The menu displays the current value of some items.

2 Click an item to toggle it on (check mark) or off (no check mark).

● In most cases, when you toggle a status bar feature on, it appears immediately.

ACTIVATE OVERTYPE MODE

1 Click Insert.

● Insert changes to Overtype, indicating that Overtype mode is on.

As you type, Word types over any existing characters that fall to the right of the cursor.

Note: You can use this same technique to activate the Macro Recording and Track Changes shortcuts.

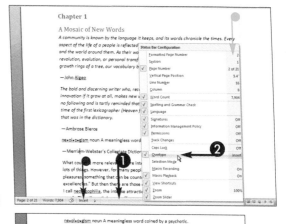

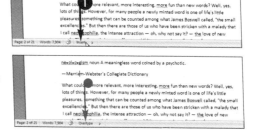

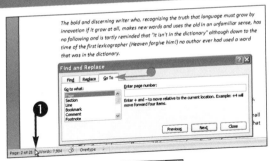

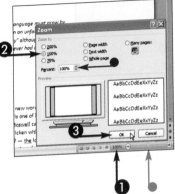

ACTIVATE FIND AND REPLACE

① Click Page Number.

● The Find and Replace dialog box appears. You can use the Go To tab to move to specific areas in a document and the Find and Replace tabs to look up and replace words.

ZOOM IN OR OUT OF PAGE TEXT

① Click Zoom.

② In the Zoom dialog box, click a Zoom option (○ changes to ◉).

● You can also click the Percent spin box to specify a magnification.

③ Click OK.

● You can also specify the magnification by clicking and dragging the Zoom slider.

Did You Know?

The Selection Mode item tells you when you are in Extend Selection mode, which offers an easy way to select a large section of text. Click at the start of the text, press F8 to enter Extend Selection mode, and then click at the end of the text. Word selects all the text between the first and last clicks. Press F8 again to end Extend Selection mode.

Register a Blog Account

You can use Word 2007 to compose and post blog entries for many of the more popular blogging sites and systems.

If you are a blogger, you most likely have to use either a Web application or a program other than Word to compose your blog posts. If you prefer Word with its powerful writing tools, you may be able to use Word 2007 to compose and

post blog entries. Word supports several blog providers, including MSN Spaces and Blogger. Word also supports blogging systems that use either MetaWebLog (such as TypePad and WordPress) or Atom (such as LiveJournal). Before you can blog, you must register a blog account with Word.

---

① Click Office.
② Click Publish.
③ Click Blog.

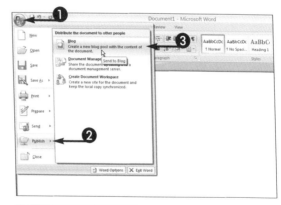

Word prompts you to register your blog account.

④ Click Register Now.

The New Blog Account dialog box appears.

⑤ Use the Blog Host list to click the blog host you use.

Note: *If you do not see your blog host, click Other.*

⑥ Click Next.

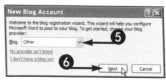

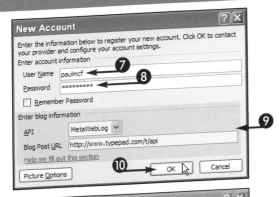

The New Account dialog box appears.

7 Type your user name.

8 Type your password.

9 Fill in the rest of the blog information.

Note: *The configuration of the New Account dialog box depends on the blog host you chose in Step 5.*

10 Click OK.

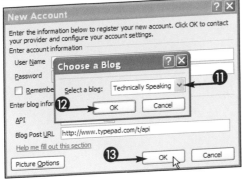

If you have multiple blogs on the host, the Choose a Blog dialog box appears.

11 Use the Select a Blog list to click the blog you want to use.

12 Click OK.

Word confirms your blog account.

13 Click OK.

More Options!
If you choose Other in Step **5**, the New Account dialog box asks you to select the blog host's API (application programming interface) and Blog Post URL. If you are not sure what to fill in, click the Help Me Fill Out This Section link. This takes you to a Web page that tells you the API and blog post URL of some common systems, including LiveJournal, TypePad, and WordPress.

With your blog account set up, you can now use Word to create a blog entry and post it to your blog host.

The advantage you get by using Word to create your blog entries is that you can use many of Word's powerful features to craft your blog posts as readily as you can any other document. When you are composing a blog post, you have access to Word's text and paragraph formatting features, styles, the proofing tools (spelling and grammar checking, the thesaurus, and so on), and you can also insert hyperlinks, tables, and images. Fortunately, Word outputs very clean HTML, so your posts are not cluttered with complex tags, as in previous versions of Word.

① Click Office.

② Click Publish.

③ Click Blog.

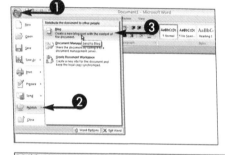

A new blog document appears.

④ Click on the [Enter Post Title Here] placeholder and type your blog post title.

⑤ Type the body of your blog post.

⑥ Click Publish.

⑦ Click Publish.

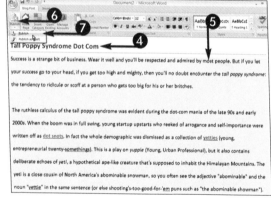

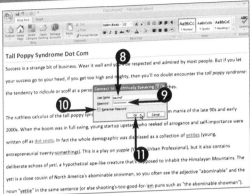

The Password dialog box appears.

8 Type your user name.

9 Type your password.

10 To avoid this dialog box in the future, click Remember Password (☐ changes to ☑).

11 Click OK.

Word publishes the blog post.

● Word displays a message at the top of the post to let you know when it was posted.

Did You Know?

After you have published a blog entry, you may find errors or want to add new material. Do not copy the material to a new blog document and publish it again, or you will end up with two versions of the post on your blog. Instead, in the Blog Post tab, click Open Existing to display a list of posts on the selected blog account. (If you have more than one account, use the Account list to select the one you want.) Click the post you want to edit and then click OK.

By default, Word keeps track of the files you work with and lists the nine most-recently used documents on the right side of the Office menu. The recent documents list offers a convenient way to quickly open your most recent work. Unless you password-protect a file, other users can also easily open and view this file if it appears on the recent documents list.

Fortunately, a method is available that you can use to remove a document from the Word Recent Documents list. Using a keyboard shortcut in conjunction with a mouse click, you can make a file disappear from the list. However, the results of this method are not permanent.

① Press Ctrl+Alt+-.

● The mouse pointer takes the shape of a minus sign.

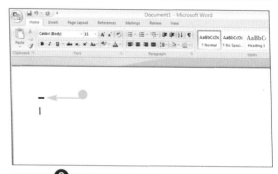

② Click Office.

③ Click the document you want to remove from the list.

Word removes the document from the list.

As any Word user knows, you can waste a lot of paper when printing out documents during editing. You can use the Zoom options found in the Print dialog box to help conserve paper consumption by printing out multiple pages on a single sheet of paper.

By default, the Print dialog box sets the Pages Per Sheet option to 1 page, which means one document page uses one sheet of printer paper. You can change this setting to print 2 pages per sheet, 4 pages per sheet, and so on, up to 16 pages per single sheet.

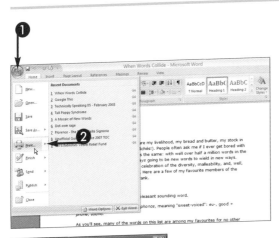

① Click Office.

② Click Print.

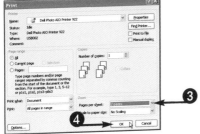

The Print dialog box appears.

③ Click here and select the desired number of pages per sheet.

④ Click OK.

Word prints out the document based on your new settings.

Navigate Long Documents Using a Table of Contents

You can use a table of contents, also called a TOC, to help you move around a long document. The TOC works by creating links to heading styles throughout your document. Styles are pre-selected formatting that you can apply to document text, such as headings and body text.

When you activate the TOC feature, Word attempts to build a table of contents by searching your document for headings and then sorting the headings based on heading levels. By default, Word includes page numbers along with the TOC headings and aligns them to the right of the heading text.

① Click in the document where you want to insert the TOC.

② Click References.

③ Click Table of Contents.

● If you want to apply a predefined TOC, click one of the TOC styles in the gallery.

④ Click Insert Table of Contents.

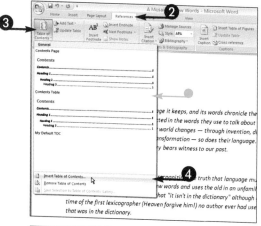

The Table of Contents dialog box appears.

⑤ Use the Formats list to click a TOC format.

● The Print Preview area shows the TOC format.

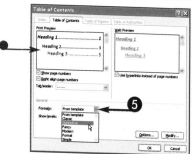

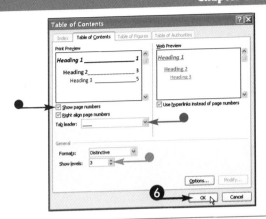

- If you want page numbers, use the Tab Leader list to click a type of leader character.

- Use the Show Levels spin box to click the number of heading levels you want in the TOC.

- Click the Show Page Numbers option (☑ changes to ☐) if you do not want page numbers to appear in the TOC.

6 Click OK.

  Word adds the TOC to the document.

- To jump to a heading, hold down Ctrl and click the heading in the TOC.

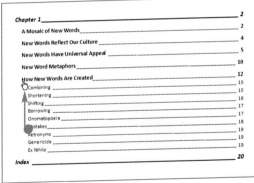

Did You Know?

To create a table of contents from custom styles that you create in Word, follow Steps **1** to **4** in this task to open the Table of Contents tab of the Index and Tables dialog box. Click Options to open the Table of Contents Options dialog box, and select the custom headings you want to use in the TOC.

Navigate Long Documents Using Bookmarks

Long documents can be difficult to navigate, especially when you are trying to locate a specific section of text. You can use a bookmark to tag a location or section of text for quick future access.

Bookmarks in Word are similar to those you use in a Web browser to mark your favorite Web pages. The bookmark

identifies a location or section of text, and by giving a bookmark a distinct name, you can use the bookmark at any time to quickly jump to that location in the document.

You can only begin a bookmark name with a letter, not a number. Also, you cannot use spaces in bookmark names.

INSERT A BOOKMARK

1 Select the text or click where you want to insert a bookmark.

2 Click Insert.

3 Click Bookmark.

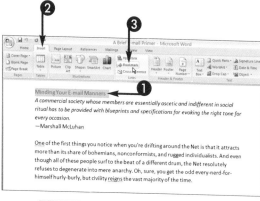

The Bookmark dialog box appears.

4 Type a name for the bookmark.

5 Click Add.

Word adds the bookmark.

LOCATE A BOOKMARK

1. Click Insert.
2. Click Bookmark.

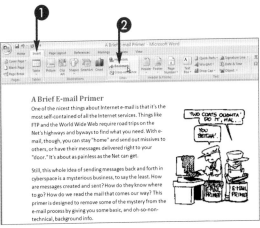

A Brief E-mail Primer

One of the nicest things about Internet e-mail is that it's the most self-contained of all the Internet services. Things like FTP and the World Wide Web require road trips on the Net's highways and byways to find what you need. With e-mail, though, you can stay "home" and send out missives to others, or have their messages delivered right to your "door." It's about as painless as sending the Net can get.

Still, this whole idea of sending messages back and forth in cyberspace is a mysterious business, to say the least. How are messages created and sent? How do they know where to go? How do we read the mail that comes our way? This primer is designed to remove some of the mystery from the e-mail process by giving you some basic, and oh-so-non-technical, background info.

The Bookmark dialog box appears.

3. Click the bookmark to which you want to jump.
4. Click Go To.

- Word displays the page containing the bookmark.

5. Click Close.

TIP

Did You Know?

You can use the Go To command to jump to various locations in a document. Click Home, click the Find menu, and then click Go To to open the Find and Replace dialog box with the Go To tab displayed. (You can also press Ctrl+G or click the page number in the status bar.) Click Bookmark in the Go To What list and then use the Enter Bookmark Name list to click the desired bookmark. Click Go To, and Word jumps to that location.

Compare Two Documents Side by Side

You can quickly and easily compare the contents of two separate documents by activating Word 2007's Compare Side by Side feature.

What do you do if you send a person a copy of a document for editing, but he or she forgets to turn on revision marks so you cannot easily see the new changes? Normally you would open both documents and then switch from one window to another or try to arrange the documents onscreen so you can see both at once. You can avoid this extra work by using the Compare Side by Side feature, where Word arranges the document window so that you can easily compare the two documents.

① Open the two documents that you want to compare.

② Switch to one of the documents.

③ Click View.

④ Click View Side by Side.

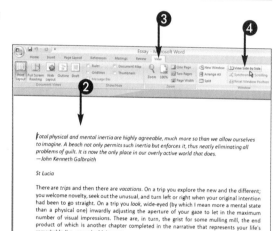

If you have three or more documents open, the Compare Side by Side dialog box appears.

⑤ Click the other document you want to include in the comparison.

⑥ Click OK.

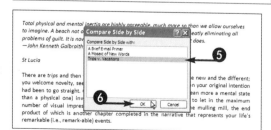

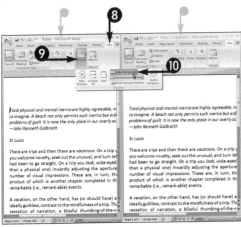

● Word displays the two
documents side by side.

❼ Compare the two
documents.

❽ When you are finished,
click View.

❾ Click Window.

❿ Click View Side by Side.

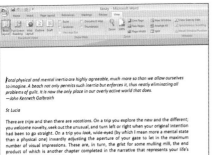

Word restores the
windows.

More Options!
One of the nicest aspects of the Compare Side by Side feature is
synchronous scrolling, which means that as you scroll up or down in
one document, Word automatically scrolls up or down by the same
amount in the other document. This makes comparing the documents
easy, but if you do not want to use this feature, you can turn it off. While
you are comparing documents side by side, click Window and then click
Synchronous Scrolling.

If you consistently retype the same text over and over again, Word enables you to add the text to the AutoText entries. Instead of typing out the whole string of words each time, AutoText lets you insert the text with just a few mouse clicks.

Word includes AutoText as a part of the AutoCorrect features. Your entry must contain at least four characters. You can also use AutoText to insert a graphic into your document.

ADD AN AUTOTEXT ENTRY

① Type and select the text you want to store as an AutoText entry.

② Click Insert.

③ Click Quick Parts.

④ Click Save Selection to Quick Part Gallery.

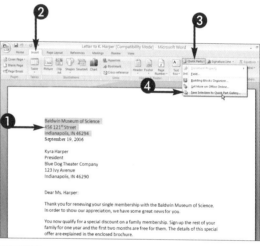

The Create New Building Block dialog box appears.

⑤ Edit the name, if desired.

⑥ In the Gallery list, click AutoText.

⑦ Type a description, if desired.

⑧ Click OK.

Word adds your entry to the AutoText list.

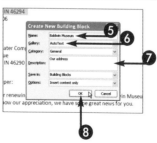

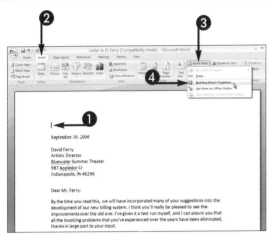

INSERT AN AUTOTEXT ENTRY

1. Click where you want the AutoText entry to appear.
2. Click Insert.
3. Click Quick Parts.
4. Click Building Blocks Organizer.

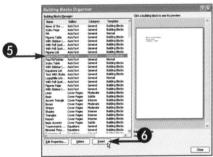

The Building Blocks Organizer dialog box appears.

5. Click the AutoText entry.
6. Click Insert.

Word inserts the AutoText and closes the dialog box.

Change It!

If you need to edit your AutoText entry, click Insert, Quick Parts, Building Blocks Organizer to display the Building Blocks Organizer dialog box. Click your AutoText entry and then click Edit Properties. Use the Modify Building Block dialog box to edit the AutoText Name, Descriptions, or other properties, and then click OK.

Keep Words Together with a Non-Breaking Space

By default, Word automatically wraps a line of text to the next line once you reach the right margin. However, this may result in an awkward breakup of a multiword phrase or a proper name. For example, if you type the name *John Smith* at the end of the line, Word may wrap the last name to the next line of text. To avoid this kind of problem, you can apply a non-breaking space to keep names and other multiword phrases together. Word breaks the line before or after the phrase or name rather than in the middle.

① Select the space after the first word in the phrase or name.

② Press Ctrl+Shift+Spacebar.

The Authenticity Problem

You might recall an infamous story from the '70s in which the sportscaster Howard Cosell was doing a Monday Night Football broadcast and received what he thought was a call from the boxer Muhammad Ali. At the time, Ali was in Zaire preparing to fight George Foreman, so this was a real coup for Cosell. In fact, he even did a brief interview with Ali right on the air to a nationwide TV audience. Much to Cosell's chagrin (not to mention his embarrassment), the call turned out to be a hoax (the caller was actually somewhere in the Midwest, I think).

This brings us to the second e-mail security problem: authentication. When you receive a message, the header's From line tells you the e-mail address of the person who sent the missive. Or does it? The Internet e-mail system is such an open book that it's ridiculously easy to forge other people's e-mail addresses! Now, obviously, if you get a message from president@whitehouse.gov or billg@microsoft.com, you can pretty well guess you're dealing with a forgery (depending on the social circles you run in). But if you get flamed by a total stranger, or if someone you know inexplicably asks for your credit card number, there's no way to tell whether the message is on the up-and-up.

● Word adds a non-breaking space.

Repeat Steps **1** and **2** for each additional space in the phrase or name.

Note: *You do not need to apply a non-breaking space to the space immediately following the last word in the phrase or name.*

The Authenticity Problem

You might recall an infamous story from the '70s in which the sportscaster Howard Cosell was doing a Monday Night Football broadcast and received what he thought was a call from the boxer Muhammad Ali. At the time, Ali was in Zaire preparing to fight George Foreman, so this was a real coup for Cosell. In fact, he even did a brief interview with Ali right on the air to a nationwide TV audience. Much to Cosell's chagrin (not to mention his embarrassment), the call turned out to be a hoax (the caller was actually somewhere in the Midwest, I think).

This brings us to the second e-mail security problem: authentication. When you receive a message, the header's From line tells you the e-mail address of the person who sent the missive. Or does it? The Internet e-mail system is such an open book that it's ridiculously easy to forge other people's e-mail addresses! Now, obviously, if you get a message from president@whitehouse.gov or billg@microsoft.com, you can pretty well guess you're dealing with a forgery (depending on the social circles you run in). But if you get flamed by a total stranger, or if someone you know inexplicably asks for your credit card number, there's no way to tell whether the message is on the up-and-up.

You can control the spacing between sentences as you type. Ordinarily, you press the Spacebar once to create a space between sentences. However, some types of documents, such as research and term papers, commonly require double spaces between sentences. If you activate the double-space rule in the Word Grammar

and Style options, you can achieve the effect of a double space between sentences without having to press the Spacebar twice. Word inserts the double space for you. This reduces your typing time and ensures consistency throughout the document.

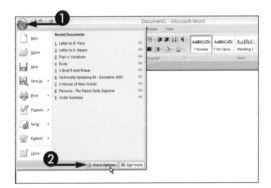

① Click Office.

② Click Word Options.

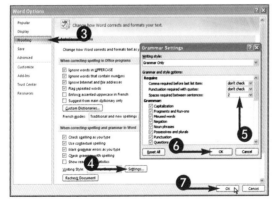

The Word Options dialog box appears.

③ Click Proofing.

④ Click Settings.

The Grammar Settings dialog box opens.

⑤ Use the Spaces Required Between Sentences list to click 2.

⑥ Click OK.

⑦ Click OK.

Word inserts a double space after every sentence.

Using the Research Pane to Translate Text

You can use the Research task pane in Word to translate a single word, a phrase, or your entire document to another language.

You can use the bilingual dictionaries that install with Word to translate single words or short phrases. For larger amounts of text, you can use machine translation on the Web. You need an Internet

connection to access the Web and utilize the machine translation services of Microsoft. When translating larger amounts of text, your Web browser opens to display the results.

---

1 Select the word or phrase you want to translate.

2 Click Review.

3 Click Translate.

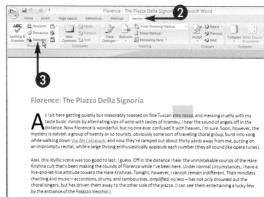

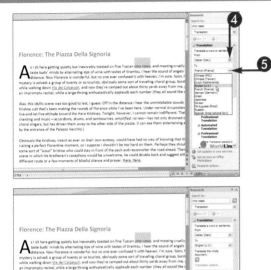

The Research task pane appears.

④ Use the From list to click the language from which you want to translate.

⑤ Use the To list to click the language to which you want to translate.

● The task pane displays the translation.

To add a translated item to your document, select the word or phrase in the pane, right-click the selection, and then click Copy. Position the cursor in your document and press Ctrl+V to paste the translated text.

Did You Know?

To quickly translate a specific word in your document, open the Research task pane and display the translation options, setting the language to which you want to translate. Press Alt and click the word you want to translate. The Research task pane immediately shows the results.

You can add line numbers that appear in the margins of your Word documents. This feature is particularly helpful for legal, medical, or insurance documents; for annotating computer programs or scripts; or for literary analysis.

When you turn on the line-numbering feature, Word displays line numbers in the left margin for every line of text in the document. You can tell Word to start at

a certain number, restart numbering for different pages and sections in your document, or to apply continuous line numbering throughout the entire document.

Word automatically renumbers for you. Because the line numbers appear in the margin, you cannot select the line numbers for editing.

---

① Click Page Layout.

② Click Line Numbers.

● If you just want basic line numbers, click Continuous and skip the rest of the steps.

③ Click Line Numbering Options.

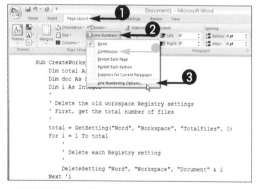

```
Sub CreateWorks
    Dim total A
    Dim doc As
    Dim i As Int
    '
    ' Delete the old workspace Registry settings
    ' First, get the total number of files
    '
    total = GetSetting("Word", "Workspace", "TotalFiles", 0)
    For i = 1 To total
        '
        ' Delete each Registry setting
        '
        DeleteSetting "Word", "Workspace", "Document" & i
    Next 'i
```

The Page Setup dialog box appears with the Layout tab displayed.

④ Click Line Numbers.

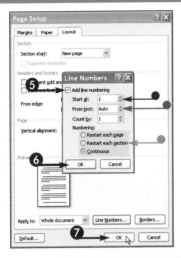

The Line Numbers dialog box appears.

⑤ Click Add Line Numbering (☐ changes to ☑).

● You can select a starting number.

● You can select the spacing between the text and the line numbers.

● You can select an option to restart numbering for each page or section, or to set continuous numbering (○ changes to ⊙).

⑥ Click OK.

⑦ Click OK.

● Word adds line numbers to the margin of the document.

```
1   Sub CreateWorkspace()
2       Dim total As Integer
3       Dim doc As Document
4       Dim i As Integer
5       '
6       ' Delete the old workspace Registry settings
7       ' First, get the total number of files
8       '
9       total = GetSetting("Word", "Workspace", "TotalFiles", 0)
10      For i = 1 To total
11          '
12          ' Delete each Registry setting
13          '
14          DeleteSetting "Word", "Workspace", "Document" & i
15      Next 'i
16      '
17      ' Create the new workspace
```

TIP

Did You Know?

To apply line numbers to a portion of the document, first select the text, and then open the Page Setup dialog box as shown in this task. Click the Layout tab, and then use the Apply To list to click Selected Text. You can now open the Line Numbers dialog box and apply the line options.

Set Off a Paragraph with a Border

You can use partial or full borders to set off a paragraph within your document.

You can also set off an entire paragraph with a border, drawing attention to the text or message.

You can use the Borders and Shading dialog box to control how a border appears around a paragraph, as well as the style of the line borders. You can choose from a variety of line styles and thicknesses, and control the color of the line borders. You can preview your border selections before applying them to the actual paragraph.

① Click inside of, or select, a paragraph to which you want to add a border.

② Click Home.

③ Drop-down the Borders tool.

● You can use the gallery to click a basic border.

④ Click Borders and Shading.

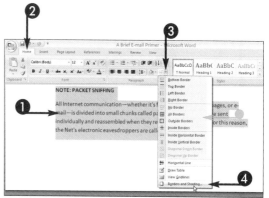

The Borders and Shading dialog box appears with the Borders tab displayed.

⑤ Click Box.

● Use the Style list to click a border style.

● Use the Color list to click a border color.

● Use the Width list to click a border width.

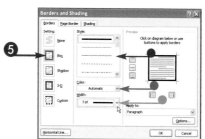

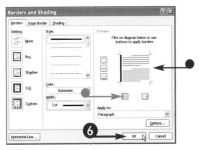

- The Preview shows your current setting and styles.

- To remove any sides of the border, you can click a border button.

6 Click OK.

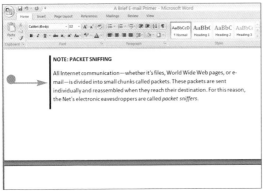

- Word applies the paragraph border.

  In this example, Word applied a partial paragraph border and indented the paragraph to create a pull-quote effect.

NOTE: PACKET SNIFFING

All Internet communication—whether it's files, World Wide Web pages, or e-mail—is divided into small chunks called packets. These packets are sent individually and reassembled when they reach their destination. For this reason, the Net's electronic eavesdroppers are called *packet sniffers*.

TIP

Did You Know?

You can apply shading to a paragraph. Shading is a color or pattern that appears behind the paragraph text. To apply shading, click the Shading tab in the Borders and Shading dialog box. Select a fill color from the Fill palette, or click More Colors to select another color. Use the Style list to click a color intensity or fill pattern.

Resume Numbering in an Interrupted Numbered List

When you use numbered lists in your Word document, you may sometimes need to interrupt the numbered list with a paragraph and then resume the list. The smart tags in Word can help you pick up where you left off. When the smart tag options are active, which they are by default, a smart tag icon appears next to the paragraph. When clicked, the smart tag, which looks like a lightening bolt, displays several options that relate to your work. In the case of numbered lists, the smart tag displays AutoCorrect options that create numbered lists.

① When you start a new paragraph to continue the numbered list, click the Home tab's Numbering button.

A smart tag appears next to the first number.

② Click the smart tag.

③ Click Continue Numbering.

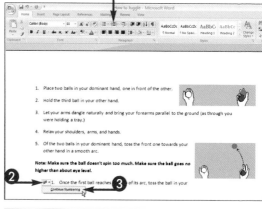

● Word resumes the numbering sequence of the previous numbered list.

To change the formatting of your numbers in a numbered list, click any number in the list and then pull down the Home tab's Numbering list and select another number style.

You can quickly insert a horizontal line across your document page using a keyboard shortcut in Word. For example, you can insert a horizontal line between two sections to act as a divider.

Ordinarily, you must go through the Borders and Shading dialog box to get to the Horizontal Line dialog box, and then specify a line type to apply. However, for a simple line, you can use a keyboard shortcut by typing three special characters. If you enter three special characters but do not want to create a line, simply activate the Undo command.

Euphonious

Pleasant sounding, especially a pleasant sounding word.

From the ancient Greek word *euphonos*, meaning "sweet-voiced": *eu-*, good + *phone*, sound.

As you'll see, many of the words on this list are among my favourites for no other reason than sheer euphony. Words such as hullabaloo, demonomania, and flibbertigibbet just roll off the tongue irresistibly. You'll also see that I'm fascinated by harsh, non-euphonious words such as crepuscular and feculent.

Portmanteau

1. A large leather suitcase that opens into two hinged compartments.

2. A word formed by merging parts of two different words.

From the French word *portemanteau*, meaning "coat carrier."

The mundane meaning of portmanteau -- a large leather suitcase -- isn't what interests me here. Instead, I prefer the second meaning: a word formed by merging parts of two different words. This usage of portmanteau comes from Lewis Carroll, in *Through the Looking Glass*. Alice is puzzling over the meaning of some of the words in the poem Jabberwocky, and asks Humpty Dumpty for help. Here's what he has to say about the word *slithy*:

"Well, '*slithy*' means 'lithe and slimy.'...You see it's like a portmanteau -- there are two meanings packed up into one word."

Euphonious

Pleasant sounding, especially a pleasant sounding word.

From the ancient Greek word *euphonos*, meaning "sweet-voiced": *eu-*, good + *phone*, sound.

As you'll see, many of the words on this list are among my favourites for no other reason than sheer euphony. Words such as hullabaloo, demonomania, and flibbertigibbet just roll off the tongue irresistibly. You'll also see that I'm fascinated by harsh, non-euphonious words such as crepuscular and feculent.

Portmanteau

1. A large leather suitcase that opens into two hinged compartments.

2. A word formed by merging parts of two different words.

From the French word *portemanteau*, meaning "coat carrier."

① Click in the document where you want to insert a line.

② Type three dashes.

③ Press Enter.

● Word inserts the line.

● You can also insert other types of lines using the keyboard. To achieve the effects you see here, type three asterisks, underscores, equal signs, pound signs, or tildes, and press Enter.

Emphasize Paragraphs with Drop Caps

You can use drop caps to add emphasis to your text or to create a dramatic effect. A drop cap is a large initial or capital letter that appears at the beginning of a paragraph.

By default, a drop cap is set up to drop three lines. This means that the height of the drop cap is equivalent to three lines

of text. You can specify how many lines down to set the drop cap. You can also specify a distance from the text. By default, the drop cap appears at zero distance from, or directly next to, the paragraph text.

The Drop Cap dialog box also allows you to change the font of the drop-cap.

---

1. Click inside the paragraph that you want to format with a drop cap.

2. Click Insert.

3. Click Drop Cap.

- If you want a basic drop cap, click Dropped or In Margin.

4. Click Drop Cap Options.

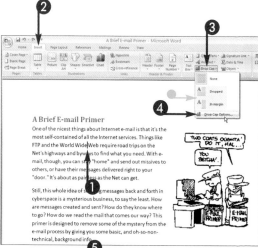

The Drop Cap dialog box appears.

5. Click the type of drop cap position you want to apply.

6. Use the Lines to Drop spin box to click or type the number of lines you want the character to drop.

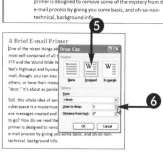

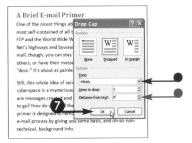

- You can use the Font list to click a font style for the drop cap.

- You can use the Distance from Text spin box to click or type the space you want between the drop cap and the paragraph text.

⑦ Click OK.

- Word applies the drop cap.

Note: *Because Word places drop caps in text boxes, you can move, resize, and apply formatting to the text box, such as a background color or a border.*

Note: *To return a drop cap to normal character text, follow Steps 1 to 3 and then click None.*

A Brief E-mail Primer

ne of the nicest things about Internet e-mail is that it's the most self-contained of all the Internet services. Things like FTP and the World Wide Web require road trips on the Net's highways and byways to find what you need. With e-mail, though, you can stay "home" and send out missives to others, or have their messages delivered right to your "door." It's about as painless as the Net can get.

Still, this whole idea of sending messages back and forth in cyberspace is a mysterious business, to say the least. How are messages created and sent? How do they know where to go? How do we read the mail that comes our way? This primer is designed to remove some of the mystery from the e-mail process by giving you some basic, and oh-so-non-technical, background info.

Did You Know?

For eye-catching drop caps, use a decorative font, such as Algerian or Old English MT. Although adding drop caps to every paragraph in a document is not a good idea, when used sparingly, they can create a good visual break for people viewing your document.

By default, comment text in your Word documents appears in 10-point type, using the same Body font as the current theme (Calibri, in the default Office theme). If you intend to create and read a lot of comments in a document, you may want to change the font and size to make the text more legible.

Word formats comment text in accordance with a preset style. A style is a set of formatting characteristics you can apply to text.

To customize comment text, you must open the Apply Styles task pane and then modify the Comment Text style.

---

① Click inside a comment.

② Press Ctrl+Shift+S.

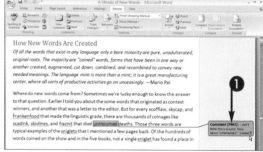

● The Apply Styles task pane appears with the Comment Text style selected.

Note: Another way to display the Apply Styles task pane is to click Home, drop down the Styles gallery, and then click Apply Styles.

③ Click Modify.

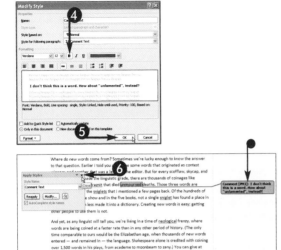

The Modify Style dialog box appears.

④ Make the changes you want to the font and font size or to other formatting options.

⑤ Click OK.

● Word applies the new comment style to existing comment text boxes as well as comments you add later.

⑥ Click Close to remove the Apply Styles task pane.

Customize It!

The Modify Style dialog box includes a wide variety of formatting options you can apply to your comment text. You can set alignment, line spacing, paragraph spacing, and indents. You can also change the font color and style, such as bold or italics. You can click Format to reveal additional categories of attributes you can apply to styles.

If your document includes graphic items, you can add captions to describe the items for the reader.

Using the Caption feature in Word, you can automatically number the captions within your document. If you move a graphic object, Word automatically renumbers captions for you. You can label captions

as figures, equations, or tables, or you can create your own labels, such as photograph or item. You can also place your captions above or below the item.

After creating a caption and a label, you can edit the caption text at any time. The caption text box works like any other text box in Word.

---

① Select the graphic object to which you want to add a caption.

② Click References.

③ Click Insert Caption.

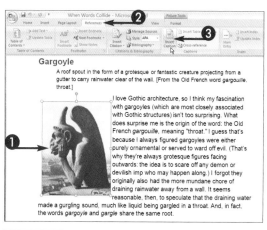

The Caption dialog box appears.

④ Use the Label list to click the label type you want.

● To create a custom label, click New Label and type in the new label text.

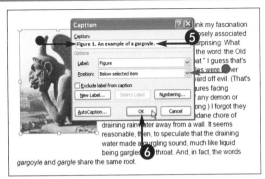

- The numbered label appears in the Caption field.

⑤ Type any additional caption text you want to include.

- You can use the Position list to click the caption position.

⑥ Click OK.

draining rainwater away from a wall. It seems reasonable, then, to speculate that the draining water made a gurgling sound, much like liquid being gargled in a throat. And, in fact, the words *gargoyle* and *gargle* share the same root.

Gargoyle

A roof spout in the form of a grotesque or fantastic creature projecting from a gutter to carry rainwater clear of the wall. [From the Old French word *gargouille*, throat.]

I love Gothic architecture, so I think my fascination with gargoyles (which are most closely associated with Gothic structures) isn't too surprising. What does surprise me is the origin of the word: the Old French *gargouille*, meaning "throat." I guess that's because I always figured gargoyles were either purely ornamental or served to ward off evil. (That's why they're always grotesque figures facing outwards: the idea is to scare off any demon or devilish imp who may happen along.) I forgot they originally also had the more mundane chore of draining rainwater away from a wall. It seems reasonable, then, to speculate that the draining water made a gurgling sound, much like liquid being gargled in a throat. And, in fact, the words *gargoyle* and *gargle* share the same root.

Figure 1. An example of a gargoyle.

- Word applies the caption to the graphic object.

  To edit the text, you can make changes directly in the caption.

Did You Know?

If you need to add callouts to an illustration you imported into Word, you can do so using Callout shapes. Click Insert and then click Shapes to display the Shapes gallery. The Callouts category of pre-drawn shapes includes 20 types of callouts. After selecting a callout shape, click where you want it go to, resize and move the shape, and reposition the line pointing to the callout.

Insert a Table from the Keyboard

Perhaps the most common method for creating a table in Word is to click Insert and then Table to display the Insert Table grid, and then drag the mouse over the number of columns and rows you want to insert. However, you can also use the keyboard to type out a table. This technique is useful if you are a fast typist and do not want to use the mouse to create a table. By typing out a string of plus and minus signs, you can start a table on any line in your document. If your table requires more rows, you can add them as you enter table cell data.

① Click where you want to insert a table.

② Type a plus sign (+).

③ Type a minus sign (-) for the number of character spaces you want to have in the first column.

④ Type a plus sign to start the next column.

⑤ Repeat Steps **3** and **4** for each column you want to add.

⑥ Press Enter after typing the final plus sign to end the last column.

● Word creates the table.

To add more rows to the table, press the Tab key after entering cell data in the last table cell.

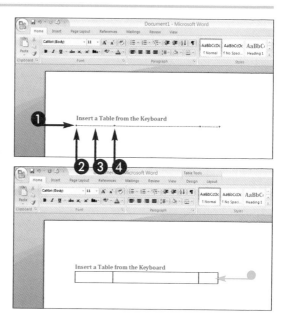

68

Column headings describe what data is in each column. If you create a long table in Word that spans more than one page, you may lose sight of your column headings as you enter data, and you may have to scroll back and forth to the top of the table to see what information each column should contain. Fortunately, Word has a technique you can use to keep column headings visible. The Repeat Row Headings command, which is only visible in Print Layout view, instructs Word to repeat the column titles for each page on which the table appears.

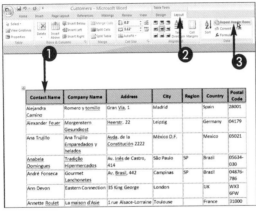

1 Click the first row containing the column headings you want to view.

2 Click Layout.

3 Click Repeat Header Rows.

● Word repeats the column headings at the top of any subsequent pages on which the table appears.

In this example, page 2 now shows column headings.

Place a Table Within a Table

Did you know that you can place tables within tables? For example, you may create a table that displays a listing of classes and professors, and a table within each class listing that displays times and room numbers. Placing a table within a table is called *nesting* a table, and it helps you further organize your document's data.

You can use the Insert Table feature to add a table within the current cell of an existing table. Either method adjusts the current table cell height and width to accommodate the new table within the existing table.

① Click inside the cell to which you want to add a table.

② Click Insert.

③ Click Table.

④ Drag across the number of columns and rows for the new table.

● Word displays a preview of the nested table.

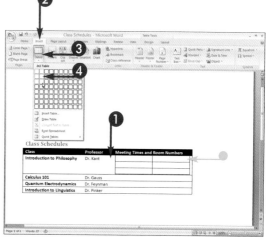

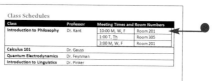

⑤ When the nested table has the number of rows and columns you want, click the mouse.

● Word inserts the new table within the existing table.

You can populate the nested table with data as needed.

If you add shapes, clip art, and other graphic objects to your document, you may find that lining them up is difficult. Word features a drawing grid that helps you position graphic objects on a page. You access the grid through the View tab.

By default, the grid does not appear when you draw customized shapes and use the AutoShapes toolbar. However, you can turn the grid on as needed, and turn it off again after you align your shapes.

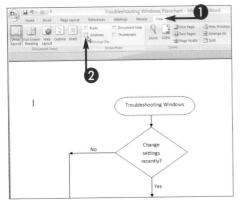

① Click View.

② Click Gridlines
(☐ changes to ☑).

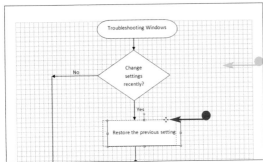

● Word displays the grid.

● You can align shapes and objects by clicking and dragging them along the gridlines.

Text boxes in Word usually contain captions for photographs and other graphic objects. You can use them in other ways to draw attention to important text. You can use text boxes to set text apart from the rest of your document and add fill colors behind the text to make the text stand out even more.

By default, text boxes include a plain white background, or fill color. You can set another fill color as well as patterns, textures, and gradient fill effects.

When selecting any type of fill, whether a solid color or a gradient effect, you should always choose colors or patterns that do not detract from the legibility of your text.

① Add a new text box, or select an existing text box.

② Click the text box edge.

Note: *Be sure to click over the edge. If you click over the text, Word inserts the cursor for you to edit the text.*

③ Click Format.

④ Click Shape Fill.

⑤ Click Gradient.

A gallery of preset gradients appears.

● To use a preset gradient, click the gradient you want and skip the rest of these steps.

⑥ Click More Gradients.

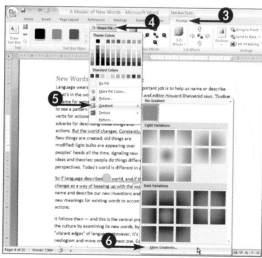

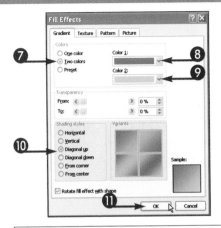

The Fill Effects dialog box appears with the Gradient tab displayed.

⑦ Click Two Colors (◯ changes to ◉).

⑧ Use the Color 1 list to click your first color.

⑨ Use the Color 2 list to click your second color.

⑩ Click the Shading style and Variant you want to use.

⑪ Click OK.

● Word applies the gradient effect to the text box background.

New Words Reflect Our Culture

Language wears many hats, but its most important job is to help us name or describe what's in the world. As the American writer and editor Howard Rheingold says, "finding a name for something is a way of conjuring its existence, of making it possible for people to see a pattern where they didn't see anything before." So we have nouns for things, verbs for actions, and adjectives and adverbs for describing those things and actions. But the world changes constantly. New things are created; old things are modified; light bulbs are appearing over peoples' heads all the time, signaling new ideas and theories; people do things differently; they look at existing things from new perspectives. Today's world is different in a thousand ways from yesterday's world.

New words give us insight into the way things are even as they act as linguistic harbingers (or canaries in the cultural coal mine), giving us a glimpse of (or a warning about) what's to come.

Apply It!

In addition to gradient fill effects, you can add a picture, texture, or pattern to the background of a text box. Follow Steps **1** to **4** to display the Shape Fill menu, and then do one of the following: click Picture to display the Select Picture dialog box; click Texture to display a gallery of textures (from which you can click one, or you can click More Textures); or click Pattern to display the Fill Effects dialog box with the Pattern tab displayed.

Watermarks are useful for documents you print and share with others. You can use a logo, text, or picture as a watermark behind your document text.

You can use graphic objects or text as a watermark. When choosing a picture as a watermark, you can apply a washout effect to make the image appear even

lighter in the background. Depending on the size of the original picture file, you can use the Scale option to resize the image.

For best results, you should use a picture that does not detract from the document text.

INSERT A PICTURE WATERMARK

① Click Page Layout.

② Click Watermark.

③ Click Custom Watermark.

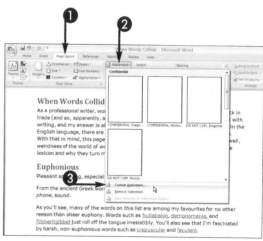

The Printed Watermark dialog box appears.

④ Click Picture Watermark (○ changes to ◉).

⑤ Click Select Picture.

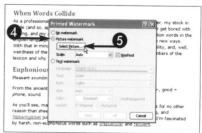

The Insert Picture dialog box appears.

⑥ Select the picture file you want to use.

⑦ Click Insert.

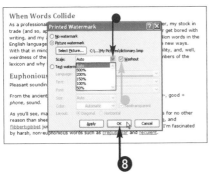

● You can click the Washout option (☐ changes to ☑) to make your picture more transparent.

● To resize the image, click the Scale list and select a size.

⑧ Click OK.

Customize It!
If your watermark picture still overpowers your document even after you apply the Washout option, you can use a graphics program, such as Adobe Illustrator or Photoshop, to increase the transparency of the image.

continued

When using text as a watermark, you can select from several presets, such as CONFIDENTIAL, DO NOT COPY, and URGENT. Word offers a dozen different preset text choices. You can also enter your own watermark text by typing directly into the Text field.

You can also control the font, size, color, and layout position of the text watermark.

You can also make the text watermark less transparent by deselecting the Semitransparent option.

Watermarks appear on every page in your document. To view a watermark, you can switch to Print Layout view mode or view the file in Print Preview mode.

● Word applies the watermark to every page in your document.

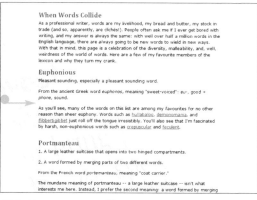

INSERT A TEXT WATERMARK

① Click Page Layout.

② Click Watermark.

Word displays a gallery of preset text watermarks.

● To use a preset text watermark, click the watermark you want to use and skip the rest of these steps.

③ Click Custom Watermark.

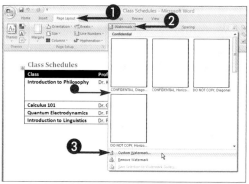

The Printed Watermark dialog box appears.

④ Click Text Watermark (○ changes to ⊙).

⑤ Use the Text field to type new watermark text.

● You can also use the Text list to click a predefined watermark.

Change any other text options you want to assign, such as Font, Size, Color, or Layout position.

⑥ Click OK.

● Word applies the text watermark to every page in the document.

Did You Know?

You can use a graphic object, such as an AutoShape, as a watermark. To do so, you must copy and paste the object into the document header. The document header appears at the top of every page. You cannot use the Printed Watermark dialog box to insert shapes and other drawn objects onto the document background. See the documentation for Word to learn more about adding headers and footers to your document pages.

Increase the Power of Your Spreadsheet with Excel

Microsoft Excel is much more than just a simple spreadsheet program. You can also use Excel to create database lists, balance a checkbook, build dynamic charts, analyze data, and so much more. Along with the basics of using the program, such as learning how to name cells, build formulas, and work with functions, you can take advantage of many other features.

This chapter offers a variety of tips and techniques you can use to make Excel work more productively for you. For example, you can learn how to tell Excel to open a particular workbook automatically every time you open the program window or how to keep your eye on a particular worksheet cell no matter where you scroll in the sheet. These techniques are handy if you revisit

the same worksheet over and over again. You can also learn tips for customizing how Excel displays gridlines, formulas, and row and column labels. You can use the text-to-speech tool to tell Excel to read back cells as you check data on a printout or ledger. You can update and retrieve stock quotes on a worksheet, or locate data from multiple sheets using the VLookup function. Other handy and timesaving techniques include freezing headings to keep your labels in view at all times, finding trends with conditional formatting, or turning Excel data into a bitmap picture that you can then insert as an illustration into another file.

Regardless of how you use Excel, this chapter is sure to offer you some nifty tricks to make building worksheets more enjoyable.

Quick Tips

By default, Excel opens a new, blank spreadsheet every time you launch the program. If you work on the same spreadsheet every time you use Excel, you can tell the program to automatically open a particular workbook for you.

To set up a workbook to open automatically, you must store the workbook file in the XLSTART folder. If you selected the default folder setting for storing Excel on your computer when you installed Excel, you can find the XLSTART folder within the following folder:

C:\Program Files\Microsoft Office\ Office12\

① Open the workbook you want to save as your default file.

② Click Office.

③ Click Save As.

The Save As dialog box appears.

④ Navigate to the XLSTART folder.

● You can use the Save In list to switch folders and drives.

⑤ Click Save.

The next time you open Excel, the workbook you saved to XLSTART opens automatically.

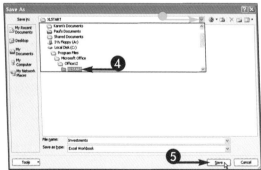

You can increase the number of files that appear in Excel's Recent Documents list. This feature gives you quick access to additional files.

By default, Excel keeps track of the nine most recent workbook files that you have used, and displays those files on the Recent Documents list, which appears on the right side of the Office menu. You can display the Office menu and click the workbook you want to open.

If you regularly use more than nine workbooks, increasing the size of the Recent Documents list gives you easy access to more of your files.

① Click Office.

② Click Excel Options.

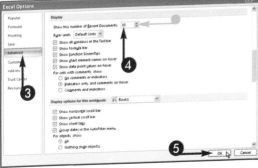

The Excel Options dialog box appears.

③ Click Advanced.

④ Type a new number in the Show this Number of Recent Documents field.

● You can also click the spin box to increase or decrease the number.

⑤ Click OK.

Excel now displays the Recent Documents list with the number of recent files you specified.

Set a New Default Font and Size

You can control the font and size that Excel automatically applies to every worksheet you open. By default, Excel applies the Arial font to all the worksheet data you enter into cells and sets the font size to 10 points.

You can change the font and size of your worksheet data as you create and use your worksheets, as well as apply any other formatting. However, you may find that establishing a default font and size before you begin adding data is easier.

You can use the Excel Options dialog box to set a new default font and size. Once you set the new font and size, every new worksheet you open utilizes the default settings.

① **Click Office.**

② **Click Excel Options.**

The Excel Options dialog box appears.

③ **Click Popular.**

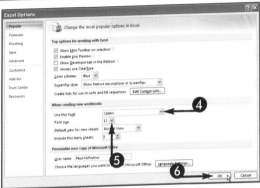

④ In the Use this Font list, click the font you want to assign.

⑤ In the Font Size list, click the size you want to assign.

⑥ Click OK.

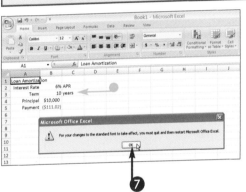

A prompt window appears, warning you that you need to restart Excel in order to use the new font and size settings.

⑦ Click OK.

You can continue working on the current worksheet, or restart Excel.

● The next time you start Excel, all new worksheets you create use the new default font and size.

More Options!
You can also change the number of worksheets that appear in each new workbook. By default, Excel creates each new workbook with three sheets. To change this, follow Steps 1 to 3, use the Include This Many Sheets spin box to specify the number of worksheets you want, and then click OK.

Essential to the structure of worksheets in any spreadsheet program, gridlines allow you to distinguish cells, columns, and rows. By default, gridlines appear in a light-gray color. You can change this color to make the lines more visible onscreen, especially if the default color is difficult to see on a worksheet.

You use the Excel Options dialog box to establish gridline color, as well as to turn gridlines on or off. Because gridlines help you to see how your cell data corresponds to column and row headings, consider leaving the gridlines feature turned on.

① Click Office.

② Click Excel Options.

The Excel Options dialog box appears.

③ Click Advanced.

④ Click Gridline Color and then click the color you want to use.

● If you want to hide gridlines instead, click the Show Gridlines check box (☑ changes to ☐).

⑤ Click OK.

● Excel applies the new color.

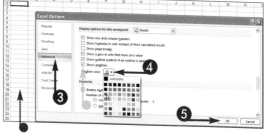

You can choose to print the worksheet gridlines along with the cell data when you print out an Excel workbook file. By default, gridlines do not print out with the data. However, by including the gridlines with the printout, you can more easily see how the row and column cells relate to each other.

Once you activate the gridline option, the gridlines print for that particular workbook. If you open another workbook and want to include the gridlines in the printout, you must activate the option again.

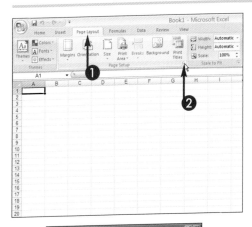

① Click Page Layout.

② Click Page Setup.

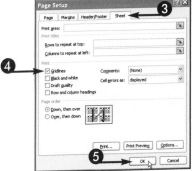

The Page Setup dialog box appears.

③ Click the Sheet tab.

④ Click the Gridlines check box (☐ changes to ☑).

⑤ Click OK.

When you print the file, the worksheet gridlines appear along with the data.

By default, Excel aligns all printed data to the left and top margins of the page, unless you specify otherwise. However, some of your worksheets may look better if you center the data on the page. You can use the Page Setup dialog box to determine how you want the printed data to align on the page. You can select the Horizontally option to center the data between the left and right margins, or the Vertically option to center the data between the top and bottom margins. You can also apply both centering alignments at the same time.

1 Click Page Layout.

2 Click Page Setup.

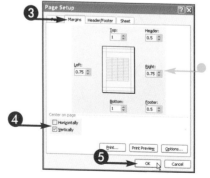

The Page Setup dialog box appears.

3 Click the Margins tab.

4 Click Horizontally or click Vertically (☐ changes to ☑). (You can also click both alignment options).

● You can also adjust the margin settings to control the page margins.

5 Click OK.

Excel centers the worksheet data on the printed page.

Print Formulas Instead of Formula Results

Ordinarily, when you print out a worksheet, you print the results of your formulas, and not the formulas themselves. However, you may occasionally want to print the formulas instead of the results.

You can use the Formulas tab to turn on the formula display option. When you activate this option, formula results do not appear in the cells containing calculations,

just the formulas themselves. Excel also highlights the cells associated with the formula, and color-codes them on the worksheet. When you print the worksheet, the formula prints as well. To view the results again, you must turn off the formula display setting in the Options dialog box.

① Click Formulas.

② Click Show Formulas.

● Excel displays all the formulas in your worksheet instead of formula results.

Note: *You can also switch between formulas and results by pressing Ctrl+`.*

③ Click Office.

④ Click Print.

Excel prints the formulas along with the other worksheet data.

Organize Worksheets by Color-Coding Tabs

You can color-code your worksheet tabs to make the task of distinguishing the contents and identity of each tab easier.

If you use multiple workbooks containing the same types of worksheets, you can apply the same tab color to the same types of worksheets to keep the worksheet data organized and easy to identify. To assign colors to your tabs, you can use the Format Tab Color dialog box, which offers a full palette of colors from which you can choose, as well as a No Color option for turning off the tab color.

---

1 Right-click the tab.

2 Click Tab Color.

3 Click a color.

● To apply a custom color, click More Colors and use the Colors dialog box to choose the color you want.

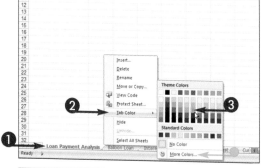

● Excel applies the color to the tab.

4 To view the color of the current tab, click another tab in the workbook.

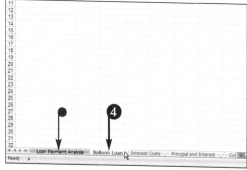

You can switch to the R1C1 reference style to make your Excel worksheets and interface compatible with those of anyone else using R1C1 style.

By default, Excel uses the A1 reference style where each cell reference is the column letter followed by the row number (such as A1 or B8). You can change to the R1C1 reference style,

where each cell is referenced by its row number followed by its column number (such as R1C1 or R8C2). When you switch to this style, Excel changes the column labels from letters to numbers.

Note that R1C1 style is absolute by default, so to make cells relative, you must add brackets to the cell numbers, as in R[5]C[8] or RC[-4].

① Click Office.

② Click Excel Options.

The Excel Options dialog box appears.

③ Click Formulas.

④ Click R1C1 Reference Style (☐ changes to ☑).

⑤ Click OK.

● Excel changes the column headings from letters to numbers.

Keep Cells in View with a Watch Window

The longer your worksheet becomes, the more difficult it is to keep important cells in view as you scroll around the worksheet. You can use the Watch Window to monitor selected cell values in your worksheet. You can even use the Watch Window to view cells in other worksheets or sheets in a linked workbook.

The Watch Window is a mini-window that floats on top of the worksheet. No matter where you scroll on the worksheet, the Watch Window always stays onscreen where you can see it. The Watch Window acts much like the Excel toolbars; you can dock it on any side of the screen.

---

① Click the cell you want to watch.

② Click Formulas.

③ Click Watch Window.

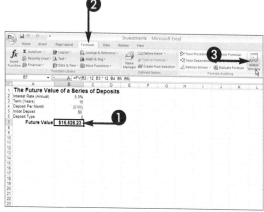

The Watch Window appears.

④ Click Add Watch.

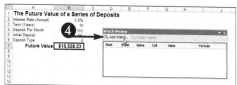

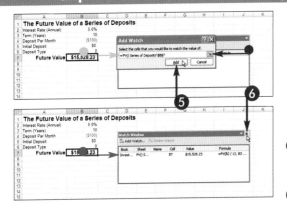

The Add Watch dialog box appears.

● The address of the selected cell appears here.

● If the address is incorrect, click Collapse Dialog and click the correct cell.

5 Click Add.

● Excel adds the cell to the Watch Window.

6 When finished with the Watch Window, click the Close button.

Excel closes the Watch Window dialog box.

Did You Know?

If you frequently use the Watch Window to monitor cells, you can use names that identify cell contents. For example, if you watch a cell range of sales totals, you can name the range Sales_Totals. Range names are more useful than default addresses, such as C12. To name any cell or range of cells, click inside the cell name box on the Formula bar, and type a name. Press Enter, and Excel saves the name. Cell and range names must start with a letter or an underscore, and cannot include spaces.

You can protect your worksheet to prevent unauthorized changes to the cells. The changes also include formatting, formulas, and layout.

To protect certain cells, you must first unlock the cells that you do not want to protect. You can use the Format menu to unlock cells.

You can now use Excel's Protect Sheet feature to establish which worksheet elements other users can change within the worksheet. You can also use the feature to assign a password to the worksheet.

① Select the cells that you do not want to protect.

② Click Home.

③ Click Format.

④ Click the Lock command to deactivate it.

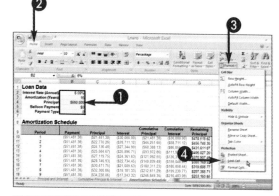

⑤ Click Home.

⑥ Click Format.

⑦ Click Protect Sheet.

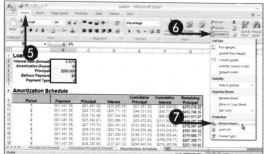

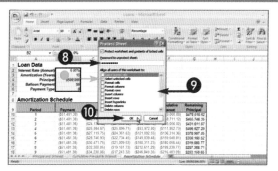

The Protect Sheet dialog box appears.

⑧ Type a password for the worksheet.

⑨ Click the items that you want other users to be able to change in the worksheet.

● In this example, users will only be allowed to select cells that are unlocked.

⑩ Click OK.

The Confirm Password dialog box appears.

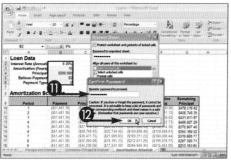

⑪ Type the password again.

⑫ Click OK.

Excel now protects the worksheet.

Did You Know?

To change protection settings for cells, you can activate the Unprotect Sheet command. However, you must know the password. To unprotect a worksheet, click Home, Format, and then Unprotect Sheet. Type the password, and click OK.

Freeze Headings for Easier Scrolling

As you work with longer worksheets, keeping your column or row labels in view is important. The longer or wider your worksheet becomes, the more time you spend scrolling back to the top of the worksheet to see which heading is which. Excel has a freeze feature you can use to lock your row or column headings in place. You can freeze them into position so that they are always in view. If you print out the worksheet, the frozen headings do not print. Row and column headings appear as they normally do, in their respective positions on the worksheet.

---

① Click View.

② Click Freeze Panes.

③ Click Freeze Top Row.

● If you want to freeze column A instead, click Freeze First Column.

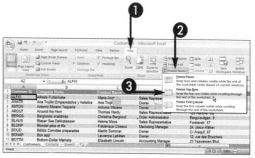

● Excel adds a solid line to set off the frozen headings.

When you scroll through the worksheet, the row or column headings remain onscreen.

To unfreeze the frozen headings, click View, Freeze Panes, and then Unfreeze Panes.

If you type a line of numbers or text that exceeds the width of a worksheet cell, the text automatically spans multiple columns. To have the text appear in a single cell, you can instruct Excel to wrap the text to the next line. Excel automatically enlarges the depth of the cell to accommodate new text lines. You use the Format Cells dialog box to activate the Wrap text option to achieve this effect.

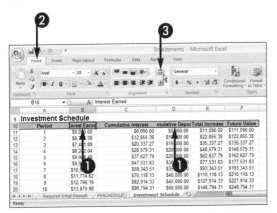

1. Select the cell or cells that you want to wrap.

2. Click Home.

3. Click Wrap Text.

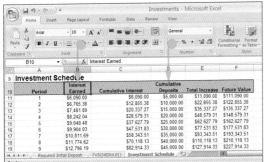

● Excel wraps the text to the next line in the cell.

Excel also increases the height of the cell row to accommodate the new text line.

You can add visual interest to your text by slanting the text upwards or downwards in the cell. You can also use this technique to make a long column heading take up less horizontal space on the worksheet.

You can make cell text angle upwards or downwards by degrees of rotation. By

default, the orientation angle is set to 0 degrees. If you set the text orientation to a positive number, such as 25, Excel angles the text in an upward direction. If you set the text orientation to a negative number, such as –40, Excel angles the text in a downward direction.

---

① Click the cell or cells containing the text you want to angle.

② Click Home.

③ Click Orientation.

● If you want to use a predefined orientation, click one of the menu items and skip the rest of the steps.

④ Click Format Cell Alignment.

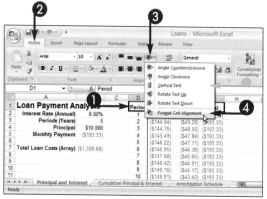

The Format Cells dialog box appears with the Alignment tab displayed.

⑤ Click an orientation marker.

● You can also use the Degrees spin box to type or click a degree of rotation.

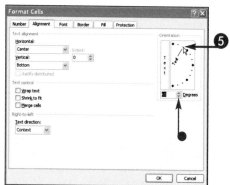

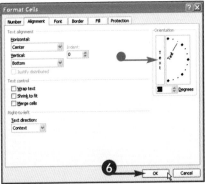

● You can click the vertical text area to display your text vertically instead of horizontally in the cell.

6 Click OK.

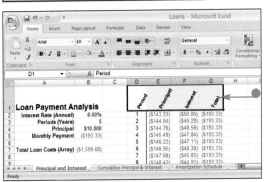

● Excel angles the cell text.

The row height automatically increases to contain the slanted text.

You can resize the column width to free up space and make your cells more presentable.

Did You Know?

If you use the Degrees spin box to set the text orientation, you can specify values in the range from 90 degrees (which is the same as clicking the Rotate Text Up command in the Orientation menu) to –90 degrees (which is the same as clicking the Rotate Text Down command).

Magnify a Selection of Cells

You can use the Zoom to Selection feature to magnify your view of any group of cells that you select in your worksheet. If you use the other zoom settings, such as 200%, Excel magnifies your view without any regard for the cells you select.

You can use the Zoom to Selection button on the Ribbon, or you can access this feature through the Zoom dialog box. However, you achieve faster results if you use the Zoom to Selection button instead of the Zoom dialog box.

① Select the cells you want to magnify onscreen.

② Click View.

③ Click Zoom to Selection.

● You can also click Zoom to open the Zoom dialog box, click Fit Selection, and then click OK.

Excel magnifies the cells you select.

● To return to the normal zoom, click View and then click 100%.

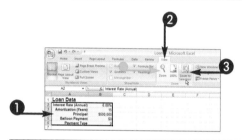

	A	B
1	**Loan Data**	
2	**Interest Rate (Annual)**	6.00%
3	**Amortization (Years)**	15
4	**Principal**	$500,000
5	**Balloon Payment**	$0
6	**Payment Type**	0
7		

You can add a background picture behind your worksheet cell data. When you add a picture to a worksheet, the image only appears on the active worksheet. The remaining worksheets in the workbook appear with the default white background.

Be sure to select a picture that does not compete with the appearance of your worksheet data.

Depending on the size of the original image, Excel may tile the picture across the background. If you do not want the image to tile, you can resize it in a graphics program.

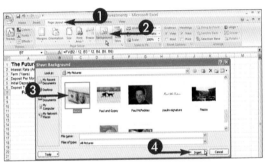
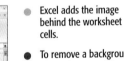

① Click Page Layout.

② Click Background.

The Sheet Background dialog box appears.

③ Select the picture file you want to use as a background.

④ Click Insert.

● Excel adds the image behind the worksheet cells.

● To remove a background you no longer want, display the worksheet, click Page Layout, and then click Delete Background.

You can make your worksheets more visually appealing by centering title text, such as a range heading, across several columns.

Using the Center Across Selection option in the Format Cells dialog box, you can achieve the same appearance as if you merged the cells. This technique leaves intersecting rows and columns safe for cutting and copying later.

① Type your title text in the leftmost cell of the range of columns.

② Select the cell and extend the selection to include the remaining cells over which you want to center the title.

③ Click Home.

④ Click Format Cells: Alignment.

The Format Cells dialog box appears with the Alignment tab displayed.

⑤ Use the Horizontal list to click Center Across Selection.

⑥ Click OK.

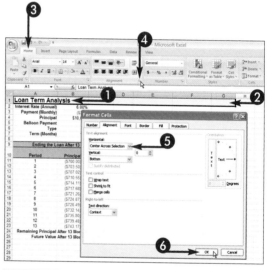

● Excel centers the text across the columns you selected.

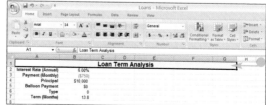

You can add comments to your formulas to explain the formula construction or purpose. For example, you can add instructions about how to use the formula elsewhere in the worksheet.

Ordinarily, when you want to add a comment to your Excel worksheet, you use comment text boxes. Comments can include anything from a note about a task to an explanation about the data that the cell contains. To add a comment to a formula, you use the N() function instead of comment text boxes. The N() function enables you to add notes about the formula within the formula itself.

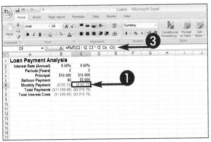

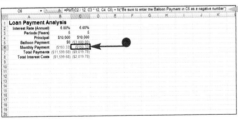

① Click the cell that contains the formula to which you want to add a comment.

② Click inside the Formula field.

③ Type **+N(**"*comment*"**)**, replacing *comment* with the comment text you want to add.

④ Press Enter.

● Excel adds the comment to the formula.

● The cell still displays only the formula results.

You can turn a group of Excel worksheet cells that contain data into a picture that you can paste into another sheet or workbook, or even into another program.

When you turn a group of cells into a picture, Excel includes the worksheet gridlines in the image by default, unless you turn off the gridlines option.

You can use the Copy Picture command to copy cells, and then the Copy Picture dialog box to select the format and appearance you want for the picture. For the best picture quality, you can select the As Shown On Screen and Picture options.

① Select the cells that contain the data that you want to turn into a picture.

② Click Home.

③ Click Paste.

④ Click As Picture.

⑤ Click Copy As Picture.

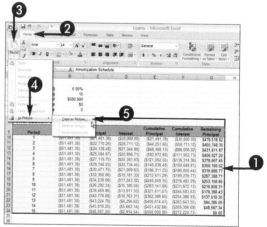

The Copy Picture dialog box appears.

⑥ Click the As Shown on Screen option (○ changes to ◉).

⑦ Click the Picture option (○ changes to ◉).

⑧ Click OK.

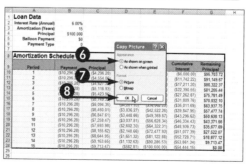

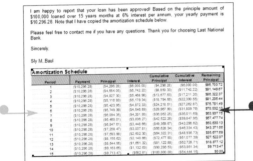

⑨ Open the worksheet or program file in which you want to paste the Excel picture.

This example pastes an Excel picture into a Word file.

⑩ Click the location where you want the picture to appear.

⑪ Press Ctrl+V.

● The Excel picture appears in the document.

● You can select the picture and click and drag the selection handles to move and resize the object.

Did You Know?

You can change the line color of or add effects to Excel data that you turn into a picture. To do so in an Office 2007 program, click the picture, click the Format tab, and then use the Picture Border and Picture Effects commands to format the picture.

Analyze Data with Conditional Formatting Graphics

You can use Excel 2007's new Conditional Formatting features to analyze your worksheet data. Conditional formatting applies different types of formatting to worksheet cells based on the data in each cell. For example, data less than a specified value might appear in a red font and data greater than that value might appear in a green font.

In Excel 2007, you can extend this type of analysis by applying graphics to each cell. With *data bars*, for example, each cell displays a colored bar, the length of which corresponds to the value in each cell. With *color scales*, each cell is shaded with a two- or three-color gradient, and the color used depends on the cell values. Finally, with *icon sets*, each cell is given an icon — such as an arrow or check mark — and the type of icon and its color depends on the cell value.

---

① Select the cells you want to format.

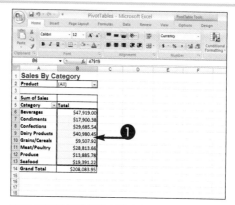

② Click Home.

③ Click Conditional Formatting.

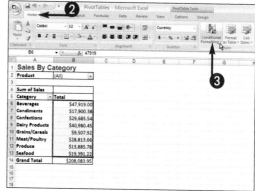

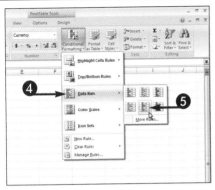

④ Click the type of conditional formatting you want to apply.

⑤ Click the predefined conditional format you want to apply.

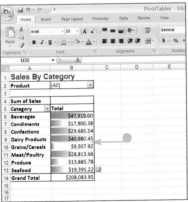

● Excel applies the conditional formatting to the cells you selected.

Did You Know?

For more control over conditional formatting graphics, follow Steps **1** to **4** and then click New Rule to display the New Formatting Rule dialog box. In the Select a Rule Type list, click Format All Cells Based On Their Values. Use the Edit the Rule Description group to specify the formatting you want to apply. Click OK when you are done.

Generate Random Numbers in Your Cells

You can use the RAND() function to generate random numbers in your worksheet cells.

After assigning the function to one cell, you can use the fill handle to populate other cells in the worksheet with more random numbers. The numbers you generate with the RAND() function take on the default numbering style for the cells. By default, Excel applies the General number format, which means that decimal numbers may appear. To limit your random numbers to whole numbers, you can open the Format Cells dialog box and set the number format to Number style and the decimal places to zero.

---

① Click the cell to which you want to add the Random function.

② Click inside the Formula field.

③ Type **=RAND()*?**, replacing *?* with the maximum random number you want Excel to generate.

④ Press Enter.

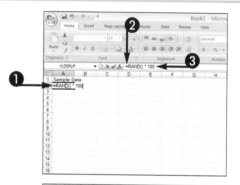

● Excel generates a random number for each cell you select.

● You can drag the fill handle across as many cells as you want to fill with random numbers.

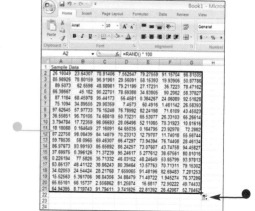

If you try to enter a fraction into a worksheet cell, Excel automatically converts the fraction into a date. For example, if you type **1/2**, Excel converts the number into the date January 2. To keep your fractions from converting, you must type a zero and press the spacebar before typing your fractions. Without the zero, Excel thinks you want to enter a date.

If you enter mixed numbers, such as **1 1/2**, Excel does not change the fraction to a date. It is only when you enter a fraction by itself that Excel converts it to a date by default.

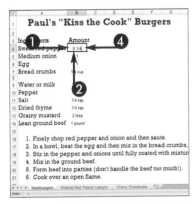

① Click the cell to which you want to add a fraction.

② Type **0**.

③ Press the spacebar.

④ Type a fraction.

⑤ Press Enter.

● Excel does not change the fraction to a date.

Retrieve a Stock Quote

You can use the Excel smart tags to download the latest quotes on your favorite stocks. You can download this stock quote data into your current worksheet or into a new sheet in your workbook. To use this feature, you must have Internet access, and you must activate the Excel smart tags.

When you enter a stock symbol and select the option from the smart tag of the cell,

Excel connects to the MSN MoneyCentral Web site to gather the latest information about the stock symbol you specify. Excel then inserts the information that it downloads into your worksheet. The information includes active links to the Web site for viewing charts, news, and looking up other stock symbols.

① Establish an Internet connection.

② Type the stock symbol into the cell using all capital letters.

③ Press Enter.

● Excel adds a small red triangle to the bottom-right corner of the cell.

④ Move the mouse pointer over the red triangle in the cell.

A smart tag appears.

⑤ Click the smart tag icon.

⑥ Click Insert refreshable stock price.

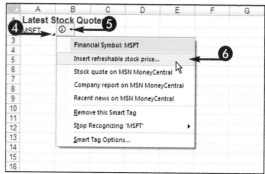

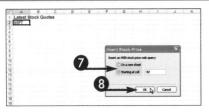

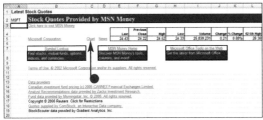

The Insert Stock Price dialog box appears.

7 Click where you want to display the stock quote (○ changes to ◉).

Click On a New Sheet to display the stock quote on a new worksheet that Excel automatically adds to the current workbook.

Click Starting at Cell to display the Stock Quote at the cell address you type in the text box.

8 Click OK.

Excel gathers the stock quote information from the MSN MoneyCentral Web site and displays it in the location you specified in Step **7**.

● You can click a link to open your Web browser and view more information.

Apply It!

To activate smart tags to use the stock quote feature, click Office, Excel Options, Proofing, and then AutoCorrect Options. In the AutoCorrect dialog box, click the Smart Tags tab, and click the Label Data with Smart Tags check box (☐ changes to ☑) and the Financial Symbol check box (☐ changes to ☑). Click OK and click OK again. You can now type a stock symbol in all caps to trigger a smart tag and look up a stock quote.

Count the Number of Days Between Two Dates

You can instruct Excel to calculate the number of days between any two dates. You must first enter the second date, and then subtract it from the first date. For example, to count the number of days between now and Christmas, enter the holiday date first, and subtract the current date from the holiday date.

If the dates are already on the worksheet, use the cell addresses in your formula. Otherwise, you must use the numeric equivalent, such as "6/21/2007" for June 21, 2007, or "5/17/2007" for May 17, 2007. You would then use the following formula to return the number of days between these dates:

="6/21/2007" – "5/17/2007"

---

① Click in the cell in which you want to insert the formula.

② Type ="date2", replacing *date2* with the second date.

③ Type –.

④ Type "date1", replacing *date1* with the first date.

⑤ Press Enter.

● Excel calculates the number of days between the two dates.

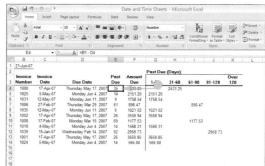

You can use the & (concatenation) operator to join text from separate cells into a text string.

When you use the concatenation operator, including spaces between the text strings is often important. For example, if you are combining first names and last names, you need a space in between to make the names readable. In the formula, you can indicate a space by entering an actual space within quotes. If the combined names require other punctuation, such as a comma, use a comma within quotes between the cell references. After establishing the formula for the first name in the list, copy the formula down the rows of the worksheet to join together the remaining names in the list.

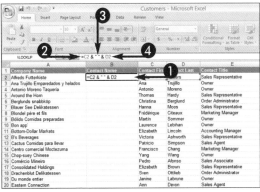

① Click inside the cell in which you want to display the text that you join together.

② Type **=text1**, where *text1* is the cell address that contains the first text string.

③ Type **& " " &** to add a space after the first text string.

④ Type **text2**, where *text2* is the cell address that contains the second text string.

Note: *Be sure to write the cell references in the order in which you want them to join together.*

⑤ Press Enter.

● Excel combines the component cell text into one cell.

You can use the Page Setup dialog box to specify page and print settings for a worksheet in your workbook.

Fortunately, you can copy the Page Setup settings from one worksheet to another and save some time. To do this, you must first group your worksheets. Using the Ctrl key, you can select the worksheets for which you want to use the same Page Setup settings and activate the settings with a single click in the Page Setup dialog box.

① Click the tab of the first sheet with which you want to work.

② Click Page Layout.

③ Click Page Setup.

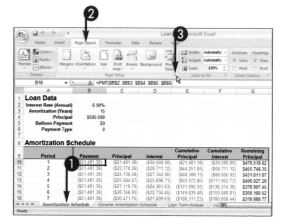

The Page Setup dialog box appears.

④ Specify the Page Setup settings that you want to assign to a worksheet in your workbook.

Note: See the Excel help files to learn more about setting up your pages with the Page Setup dialog box.

⑤ Click OK.

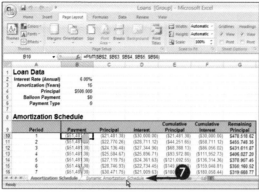

6️⃣ Press and hold the Ctrl key.

7️⃣ Click the tab of the worksheet to which you want to copy the Page Setup settings.

● Excel highlights both worksheet tabs to indicate that group mode is active.

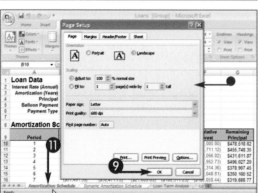

8️⃣ Repeat Steps **2** and **3**.

● Excel copies the settings from the first sheet to the Page Setup dialog box.

9️⃣ Click OK.

Excel applies the same Page Setup settings to the second worksheet.

🔟 Press and hold the Shift key.

⓫ Click the current worksheet.

Excel turns off group mode.

Did You Know?

You can also use the Page Setup dialog box to create header and footer text that appears at the top and bottom of your worksheet printouts. Open the Page Setup dialog box and click the Header/Footer tab. Click Custom Header or Custom Footer, and select from the available built-in fields buttons. Click OK to add your selections to the Page Setup dialog box. Click OK to exit Page Setup.

You can use the VLookup function to look up values vertically in a table.

To perform this technique, you must create a table that holds the values you want to look up. You must also make sure the value labels appear in the left-most column of the worksheet. To build the formula, you must reference the lookup_value, the table containing the lookup data, which is called the table_array, and a column index number, col_index_num. In the following example, the lookup value is a quantity of units ordered (column A), and the lookup table is a schedule of price discounts located to the right of the orders list. Because the value you want in the lookup table is in the second column, the column index number is 2.

① Click the cell in which you want the lookup results to appear.

② Click the Function Wizard button in the Formula bar.

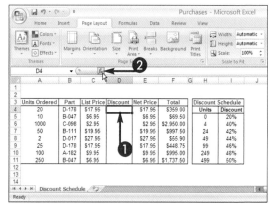

The Insert Function dialog box appears.

③ Select the Lookup & Reference category.

④ Click VLOOKUP.

⑤ Click OK.

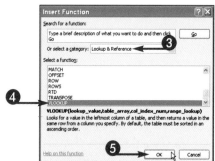

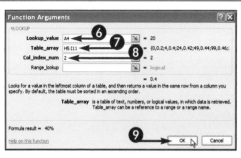

The Function Arguments dialog box appears.

6 Click the Lookup_value field and click the cell containing the value you want to look up.

In this example, the value is 200 units.

7 Click the Table_array field and select the lookup table you want to search.

To select a cell or cell range from another sheet, click the sheet tab and select the range.

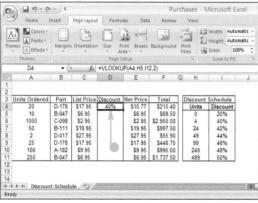

8 Click the Col_index_num field and type the column number where Excel can find the corresponding value.

In this example, Discount value is in the second column of the lookup table, so the number 2 appears in the field.

9 Click OK.

● Excel calculates the results.

Did You Know?

You can also use the HLookup function, which stands for horizontal lookup, to look up data horizontally across a table. It works the same way as VLookup, except that you specify a row_index_num, which is the row number of the value you want to return from the lookup table.

Enhance Your PowerPoint Presentations

PowerPoint is an excellent tool for communicating all types of ideas and visuals to an audience. You can create a variety of different kinds of slide show presentations, including presentations you can display on the Web. Whether you are explaining a marketing strategy to your coworkers, or just presenting a book report to your class, PowerPoint offers you all the tools necessary to present a dynamic, eye-catching slide show.

One reason for the popularity of PowerPoint is that it is such an easy program to use. It comes with a variety of slide designs and layout templates, so all you have to do is add your own text and images. However, if you want your slide shows to stand out, you need to tap into

some of the more advanced features of the program, such as the animation effects, transition controls, and drawing tools.

The tasks in this chapter introduce you to ways to speed up your workflow as well as enhance the appearance of your presentations. For example, you can reduce your presentation file size by compressing graphics, or you can turn slides into bitmap images that you can use to illustrate other files.

Because PowerPoint is so visual, getting distracted by all the visual items you can add to your presentation and thereby losing the focus of your original message is easy to do. When applying various techniques, make sure you do not overwhelm your audience and distract from your presentation message.

Quick Tips

Turn a Word Outline into a PowerPoint Presentation

You can turn an existing Word outline into a slide show in PowerPoint.

PowerPoint converts your Word document into a simple presentation. PowerPoint interprets a Heading 1 style as a top-level item in a presentation outline. Each time PowerPoint comes across Heading 1 text, it starts a new slide and the text associated with the Heading 1 style becomes the title of the slide. PowerPoint interprets a

Heading 2 style as a second-level item in a presentation outline. So each paragraph of Heading 2 text becomes a main bullet (or subtitle) in the presentation.

PowerPoint does not assign slide designs or layouts. It is up to you to add formatting and slide designs, and to illustrate the slides with any graphic items, such as clip art, shapes, or photos.

---

① Click Office.

② Click Open.

The keyboard shortcut for displaying the Open dialog box is Ctrl+O.

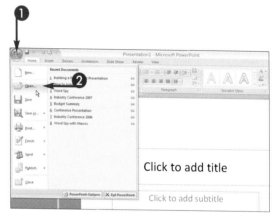

The Open dialog box appears.

③ Use the Files of Type list to click All Outlines.

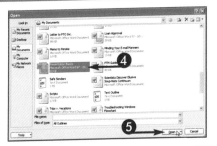

④ Locate and select the Word document you want to convert into a slide show.

⑤ Click Open.

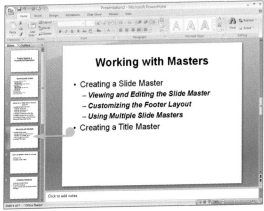

● PowerPoint converts the content of the file into a presentation and lists each slide in the Slides pane.

Did You Know?

Another method you can use is to start a new presentation and then display the Outline pane. Click Home, click New Slide, and then click Slides from Outline. In the Insert Outline dialog box, click the Word file, and then click Insert. Note that PowerPoint will not convert the Word document if it is open elsewhere, so be sure to close it before attempting to import the outline.

Convert a Slide into an Image

You can use the Save as Picture command to turn a single slide into an image, which you can then use as a graphic object in other programs, including the Office applications.

To use this technique, you display the slide you want to convert in the Notes Page view, where the PowerPoint slide appears as an image by default. You can then run the Save as Picture command to save the slide image as a separate graphics file. Once you have done that, you can then paste the image file into another program, use it on a Web site, or insert it into another slide as a graphics file.

---

① Click View.

② Click Notes Page.

PowerPoint switches to Notes Page view mode.

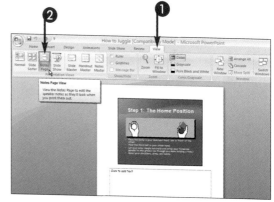

③ Right-click over the slide image.

④ Click Save as Picture.

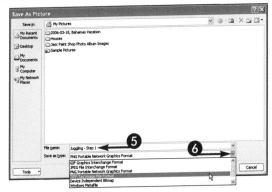

The Save As Picture dialog box appears.

⑤ Type a name for the image file.

⑥ Use the Save as Type list to click a graphic file format.

⑦ Click Save.

PowerPoint saves the slide as a graphic file for reuse in other programs.

Did You Know?

If the slide you want to convert to an image uses complex colors and fine detail, you can preserve the image fidelity by selecting the TIFF (Tag Image File Format) file type. If you plan on using the image on a Web page or in an e-mail message, compressing the image to make it smaller is best. In that case, select the JPEG file type.

Repeatedly Draw the Same Shape

If you need to draw the same type of shape multiple times, you can make this task easier by locking the shape in drawing mode.

Ordinarily, when you select a shape on the Insert tab, the tool is active for one-time use only. For example, when you click the Arrow tool button, you can draw a single arrow onscreen, after which the tool

becomes inactive again. If you want to draw another arrow, you must reselect the Arrow tool button. However, you can use a shortcut technique to keep the same drawing tool active until you decide you no longer want to draw the shape or line. This is known as locking the tool in drawing mode.

① Click Insert.

② Click Shapes.

③ Right-click the shape you want to keep active.

④ Click Lock Drawing Mode.

In this example, the Rounded Rectangle shape is selected.

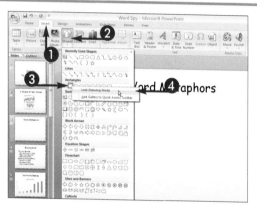

⑤ Draw the shape on the slide.

● The tool remains active on the toolbar.

⑥ Draw the shape again elsewhere on the slide.

● You can continue drawing the same object repeatedly on the slide.

⑦ Click the shape tool button you activated in Steps **3** and **4** again to deactivate the tool.

Note: *You can also deactivate the tool by selecting another drawing tool.*

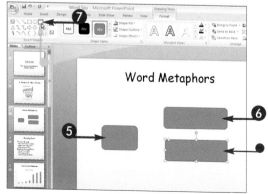

You can automatically duplicate shapes and space them evenly on a slide. Using this shortcut technique, you can duplicate an existing shape, position it where you want it to go, and then continue to repeatedly duplicate the same shape.

You can use this technique to duplicate shapes you draw with the Insert Shapes tools, as well as objects you insert such as pictures, clip art, text boxes, and WordArt objects.

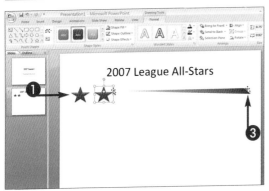

① Click the shape or object you want to duplicate.

② Press Ctrl+D.

PowerPoint duplicates the shape.

③ Drag the duplicate shape to move it and establish the spacing you want for the duplicate objects.

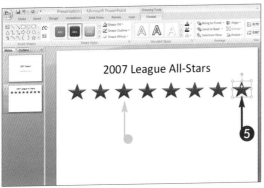

④ Press Ctrl+D.

PowerPoint duplicates the shape and the spacing you set in Step **3**.

⑤ Repeat Step **4**.

PowerPoint duplicates the shape and the spacing you want each time you perform Step **5**.

Add Connector Lines to Objects

You can use connector lines to connect slide objects. *Connector lines* are lines that PowerPoint automatically draws for you between two objects. Connector lines allow you to establish links between various objects on a slide, much like flowchart elements show links to each other. You can use connector lines to create your own version of a flowchart or diagram.

Connector lines come in several different styles. After you add a connector line between two slide objects, you can move either or both objects, and the connector line resizes to maintain the connection between them. You can also add formatting to connector lines.

① Display the slide containing the two objects you want to connect.

Note: *You can connect shapes, text boxes, WordArt, clip art, pictures, and more.*

② Click Insert.

③ Click Shapes.

The Shapes gallery appears.

④ In the Lines section, click the connector style you want to apply.

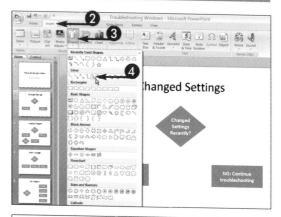

⑤ Move the mouse pointer over the first item.

● Red connector handles surround the object.

⑥ Click the handle you want to use as the anchor point.

PowerPoint establishes the handle you click as the first anchor point.

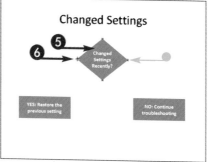

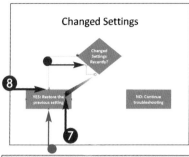

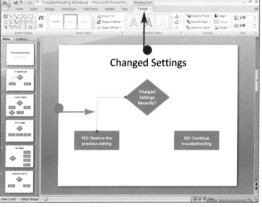

- PowerPoint adds the basic connector shape to the slide.

⑦ Drag the other end of the connector over the object to which you want to connect.

  A dashed line trails your connector line as you drag to the other object on the slide.

- Red connector handles surround the object.

⑧ Click the handle you want to use as the second anchor point.

- PowerPoint draws a connector line between the two objects.

- You can apply formatting to the connector line using the drawing tools.

TIP

Did You Know?
If you prefer the look of the Shape feature's Block Arrows, which have a chunkier style and can curve, you can use them to simulate connectors. However, you establish the connections between two objects by drawing the shapes yourself. No red connector handles appear to assist you, and if you move a slide object, the Block Arrow shape does not resize to maintain the connection between the items.

You can compress pictures in your PowerPoint document to reduce the file size of the presentation. The more pictures you add to illustrate your slides, the larger your presentation file size becomes.

The Compress Pictures dialog box displays options for reducing image resolution,

discarding the cropped areas of an image, and compressing the image file size.

Depending on the image type, you can compress a particular image on a slide, or you can choose to compress all the images in the presentation.

---

① Click the picture you want to compress.

② Click Format.

③ Click Compress Pictures.

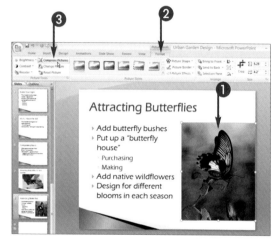

The Compress Pictures dialog box appears.

④ Click Apply to Selected Pictures Only (☐ changes to ☑) to compress only the picture you selected.

Note: If your presentation has many pictures, you might prefer to compress all of them. In that case, leave the Apply to Selected Pictures Only check box deactivated.

⑤ Click Options.

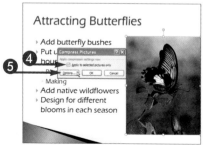

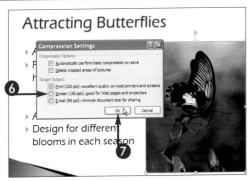

The Compression Settings dialog box appears.

⑥ Click a resolution (○ changes to ◉).

⑦ Click OK.

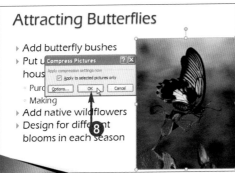

⑧ Click OK.

PowerPoint compresses the image.

Did You Know?

You can control how much compression PowerPoint applies by using the following Target Output options in the Compression Settings dialog box:

● **Print (220 ppi).** Click this option to maintain picture quality by using the least compression.

● **Screen (150 ppi).** Click this option if you will be sharing the presentation on the Web or over a network.

● **E-mail (96 ppi).** Click this option if you will be sharing the presentation via e-mail.

Create Better-Looking Shadowed Text

Although you can apply a simple text shadow effect using the Home tab's Shadow button, you can get much greater control over the text shadow by using the Text Effects menu's Shadow feature.

With the Shadow feature, you can choose from more than 20 preset shadow effects.

You can also control the color of your shadow, and perform precise adjustments for the shadow transparency, size, and blur. You can also set the exact angle that the shadow makes from the text as well as set the exact distance of the shadow from the text.

1 Select the text or text box to which you want to apply the shadow effect.

2 Click Home.

● If the text already has a shadow, click the Shadow button to remove it.

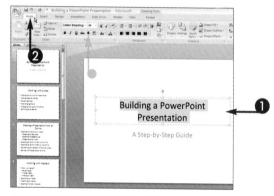

3 Click Shape Effects.

4 Click Shadow.

A gallery of preset shadows appears.

● If you want to use a preset shadow, click the style you want and skip the rest of these steps.

5 Click Shadow Options.

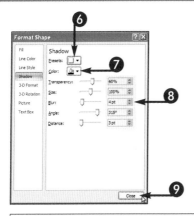

The Format Shape dialog box appears.

6 If you want to start with a preset shadow, click Presets and then click the shadow style you want.

7 Click the Color button and then click the color you want to use for your shadow.

8 Use the spin boxes to set the other shadow options you want.

9 Click Close.

● PowerPoint applies the shadow effect.

To turn off the shadow effect, repeat Steps **1** to **4** and then click No Shadow.

Building a PowerPoint Presentation

A Step-by-Step Guide

Did You Know?

Shades of the color gray make the best types of shadow effects in PowerPoint. To maintain text legibility, choose a shadow color that appears lighter than the text color. If you choose too dark a color, you cannot really see a shadow effect, but your text letters appear thicker instead.

Turn a Photo into a Slide Background

You can turn a photo into a slide background to use throughout your presentation.

The key to using a photo as a background is to make sure that the photo details or appearance do not distract the audience from viewing the message text on your slide. PowerPoint imports photos as is. The Background feature does not offer a setting for making your photo more transparent after you import it. If the photo is too dark or has too much detail, you may need to change the text box objects on each slide. For example, you can choose a more legible font or color for the slide text, or assign a fill color to the text objects to make your text stand out from the photo background.

① Click Design.

② Click Background Styles.

③ Click Format Background.

The Format Background dialog box appears.

④ Click Picture or Texture Fill (○ changes to ◉).

⑤ Click File.

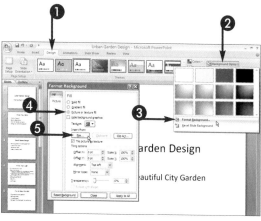

The Insert Picture dialog box appears.

⑥ Locate and select the picture you want to use as a background.

⑦ Click Insert.

PowerPoint inserts the
figure into the Picture
tab list.

8 Click Close.

● You can click Apply to
All to use the photo as
the background for all the
slides in your presentation.

Urban Garden Design

Creating a Beautiful City Garden

PowerPoint applies
the photo to the slide
background.

Apply It!

You can add a fill to any text box to make your text stand out from the
slide background. By default, all text objects you add are set to No Fill
status. To change this setting, click the edge of a text object, click Format,
and then click Shape Fill. Click the color you want to use as the fill. You
can also click Picture to insert an image from the Insert Picture dialog
box, Gradient to apply a color gradient, or Texture to apply a texture fill.

Create a Custom Color Theme

You can ensure that your slides have the look you want by creating a custom color theme.

PowerPoint comes with a number of built-in color themes that cover a dozen different slide elements. The most important of these elements are these four:

• **Text/Background 1.** Dark is the dark text color that PowerPoint applies when you choose a light background color.

• **Text/Background 2.** Light is the light text color applied when you choose a dark background color.

• **Text/Background 3.** Dark is the dark background color applied when you choose a light text color.

• **Text/Background 4.** Light is the light background color applied when you choose a dark text color.

Other slide elements cover accents such as chart markers and the color of hypertext links.

DEFINE A CUSTOM COLOR THEME

1 Click Design.

2 Click Colors.

3 Click Create New Theme Colors.

The Create New Theme Colors dialog box appears.

4 For each of the Text/Background lists, drop down the color palette and click a color.

● These images show you how the colors will appear.

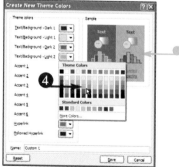

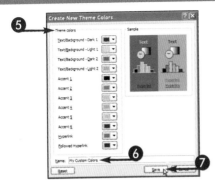

⑤ Use the lists for the other theme colors to display the palettes, and click the colors you want to use.

⑥ Type a name for your custom color theme.

⑦ Click Save.

APPLY A CUSTOM COLOR THEME

① Click Design.

② Click Colors.

③ Click your custom color theme.

PowerPoint applies the colors to the slides in the current presentation.

Did You Know?

You can use a similar technique to create custom theme fonts. PowerPoint defines a number of built-in theme fonts that specify the font used for headings (titles) and the slide body (regular text). To create a custom theme font, click Design, click Fonts, and then click Create New Theme Fonts. In the Create New Theme Fonts dialog box, click a Heading Font, click a Body Font, type a Name, and then click Save.

133

Enhance Presentations with Movies

You can add pizzazz to your presentations by including short movies that you play during a slide show.

Most PowerPoint slides present a static display of text, images, and other content. This type of presentation is usually desirable because dynamic content can distract your audience. However, for some variety it is often useful to add dynamic content such as a movie file.

PowerPoint supports several movie formats, including Windows Media File (.asf), Windows Video File (.avi), MPEG (.mpg), and Windows Media Video File (.wmv). After you insert the movie file, you can set other options such as when the movie starts, having the movie loop until it is stopped, and so on.

---

① Display the slide to which you want to add the movie.

② Click Insert.

③ Click Movie.

④ Click Movie from File.

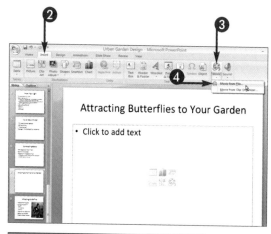

The Insert Movie dialog box appears.

⑤ Click the movie file you want to insert.

⑥ Click OK.

PowerPoint asks when you want the movie to play.

7 Click When Clicked.

● If you want the movie to start as soon as you navigate to this slide, click Automatically, instead.

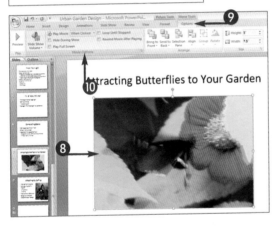

PowerPoint inserts the movie file.

8 Click the movie.

9 Click Options.

10 Use the controls in the Movie Options group to configure the movie playback.

The next time you run the slide show, the movie plays when you click it.

More Options!

In the Movie Options group (follow Steps **8** to **9** to display it), click to activate the Loop Until Stopped check box if you want the movie to play continuously until you click the movie to stop it; click to activate the Play Full Screen check box if you want the movie to take over the entire screen during playback; and click to activate the Rewind Movie After Playing check box to return the movie to the first frame after it ends.

Create Scrolling Credits

You can create the illusion of scrolling credits at the beginning or end of your slide show.

You can control the speed of the effect and whether the animation plays automatically or with a mouse click.

To create this effect, you must place a text box outside the actual slide parameters. By placing the text box above the top of the slide, you can ensure that the text appears to scroll completely off the top of the slide.

---

① Display the slide to which you want to add scrolling credits.

② Click Insert.

③ Click Text Box.

④ Draw a text box above the top of the slide.

● You can use the Zoom feature to zoom out, which allows you more room to draw the text box above the slide.

⑤ Type your credits text.

● You can use the Format tab to apply formatting to the text box.

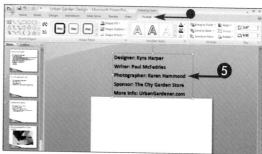

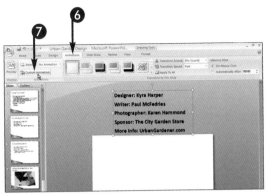

6 Click Animations.

7 Click Custom Animation.

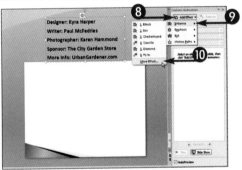

The Custom Animation pane appears.

8 Click Add Effect.

9 Click Entrance.

10 Click More Effects.

Did You Know?

To create a text box that accommodates the text you type, simply click where you want the text box to appear and start typing. As you type, the text box width increases. If you press Enter, the text box depth increases. To define the size of the text box, draw the text box by clicking and dragging. Any text you type stays within the borders you define.

continued

Just because you place a text box outside of the slide's parameters does not mean that the text box is not part of the slide. Although the text box is not actually visible on the slide itself, the scrolling text you create within the text box is clearly visible on the slide during the animation effect.

Although the text box does not sit directly on the slide, the text you type into it is still a part of the slide show.

By default, the Crawl In effect makes the text crawl from the bottom to the top. However, you can choose any direction, including from the top, bottom, left, or right.

The Add Entrance Effect dialog box appears.

⓫ Click Crawl In.

PowerPoint previews the effect.

⓬ Click OK.

⓭ Use the Start list to click when you want the effect to begin.

Click the On Click item to begin the effect when you click the slide.

Click the With Previous item to begin the effect as soon as the previous effect in the list begins.

Click the After Previous item to begin the effect as soon as the previous effect in the list is finished.

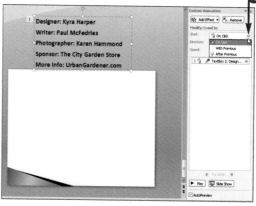

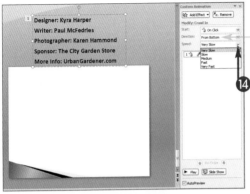

● PowerPoint selects the From Bottom direction by default.

⑭ Use the Speed list to select a speed.

To make your credits scroll slowly, click Very Slow.

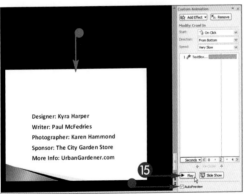

⑮ Click Play.

● To see the effect onscreen, you must click the AutoPreview check box (☐ changes to ☑).

● PowerPoint plays the animation effect.

Did You Know?

To slow down the scrolling effect, add blank lines between the credits in the credits text box. Keep in mind that this enlarges the overall size of the text box and that you may need to move it again to keep it outside the slide parameters.

Launch a Mini Slide Show Window

You can launch a mini slide show to quickly see how your edits affect the show.

When you use the mini slide show window, you can switch back and forth between the mini slide show window and the main PowerPoint program window. With this shortcut technique, you can view a miniature version of your slide show, yet still access the PowerPoint window and all the editing commands and features whenever you want. You can leave the mini slide show window open and view your edits as soon as you make them. The mini slide show window stays open until you close it.

① Click View.

② Press and hold the Ctrl key.

③ Click Slide Show.

● A mini slide show window appears.

● You can use the same controls for advancing slides as you do in full-screen view mode.

If the mini slide window is active, you can press Esc to close the window.

Ordinarily, PowerPoint 2007 stores any presentations with a .pptx file extension, which requires you to open the PowerPoint program window. However, you can save your PowerPoint presentation in the PowerPoint Show, or PPS, file format,

to make it start automatically when you double-click the filename in Windows Explorer. By saving the presentation file as a PPS file type, you avoid opening the PowerPoint program window to launch the show.

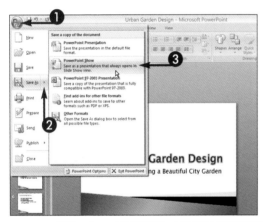

① Click Office.

② Click the Save As arrow.

③ Click PowerPoint Show.

The Save As dialog box appears.

④ Click Save.

PowerPoint saves the file.

You can double-click the file in the folder in which you store it to launch the show.

Create a Custom Slide Theme

You can create a custom slide theme that applies your own colors, fonts, and effects to a presentation.

PowerPoint comes with 20 built-in themes that you can apply to the slides in your presentation. Each theme has three components: the colors used by the slide text, background, links, and accents; the fonts used by the slide heading and body;

and the effects used by the slide objects. Applying a theme ensures a consistent look among all of your slides.

If none of the built-in themes are suitable, you can create your own custom theme that includes custom colors, fonts, and effects. You can save this theme and apply it to any presentation.

DEFINE A CUSTOM SLIDE THEME

1. Click Design.

2. Use the Colors list to click a set of colors for the custom theme.

Note: For more information about custom theme colors, see "Create a Custom Color Theme."

3. Use the Fonts list to click a set of fonts for the custom theme.

4. Use the Effects list to click a set of effects for the custom theme.

5. Click More.

● The Themes gallery appears.

6. Click Save Current Theme.

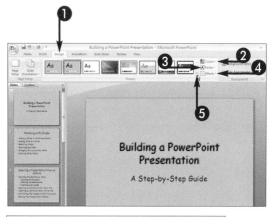

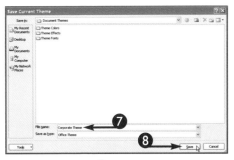

The Save Current Theme dialog box appears.

⑦ Use the File Name text box to type a name for the theme.

⑧ Click Save.

PowerPoint saves the theme.

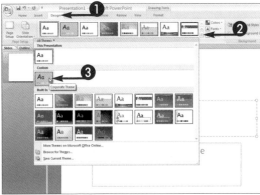

APPLY A CUSTOM SLIDE THEME

① Click Design.

② Click More.

③ Click the custom slide theme.

PowerPoint applies the custom theme to the current presentation.

More Options!
When you click a theme in the Themes gallery, PowerPoint applies the theme colors, fonts, and effects to every slide in the current presentation. If you only want to apply the theme to some of the slides in the presentation, first select those slides. Then display the Themes gallery, right-click the theme you want to use, and then click Apply to Selected Slides.

Customize and Optimize Outlook

One of the handiest organizing tools available, Outlook lets you easily work with and manage e-mail messages. You can also use it to keep track of appointments and other scheduled events, manage information about all the people with whom you interact, record and manage tasks you need to accomplish, create notes, and more. You may use all of the features of Outlook, or focus on a few key features, such as e-mail and the calendar. Regardless of how you use the program, you can always make your work easier with a few shortcuts and timesaving techniques. As with all of the Office programs, you can find your own favorite shortcuts by right-clicking on various features. When you right-click, a shortcut menu of related commands appears, and you can quickly make a selection.

Unlike the other Microsoft Office 2007 programs, Outlook has not undergone significant interface changes from previous versions. Except for the message composition window, which uses a subset of the new Word interface, Outlook 2007 looks similar to Outlook 2003 and includes many of the same features. The biggest change in Outlook 2007 is stronger security against viruses and fraudulent messages, and an improved junk e-mail filter.

This chapter shows you several ways to customize the program as well as introduces a few features that are not well known. For example, did you know you can look up an online Web map for any address in your Contacts folder? Or that you can turn that same contact's address into an envelope or label? Outlook also works intuitively with Word. For example, if you type a person's name in Word, a smart tag appears with options for adding the name to the Outlook contact list.

Quick Tips

Send Message Replies to Another Recipient

You can set up Outlook to send message replies to another person.

When you apply this feature to an outgoing e-mail, Outlook ensures that the replies you would normally receive in your Inbox are redirected to another e-mail address. Using the Message Options dialog box, you can specify an e-mail address from your Address Book, or you can manually enter another address in the field.

After specifying a different e-mail address, you can close the Message Options dialog box and send your e-mail. This feature only applies to the outgoing message you compose. To apply this feature to another e-mail, you can repeat the following steps.

---

① Compose a new e-mail message.

② Click Options.

③ Click Direct Replies To.

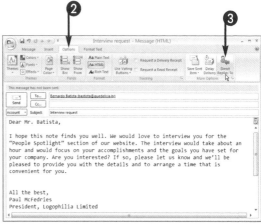

The Message Options dialog box opens.

● Outlook automatically inserts your name.

④ To send replies to someone in your Address Book, click Select Names.

You can also type the e-mail address to which you want the replies sent directly in the field.

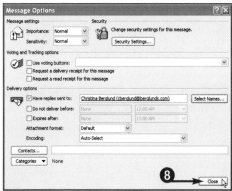

The Have Replies Sent To dialog box opens.

5 Double-click the name of the person to whom you want the replies sent.

● Outlook adds the name to the Reply To field.

6 Click your name and press Delete.

7 Click OK.

Note: *You cannot have message replies sent to a distribution list.*

8 Click Close.

You can now send the message.

Message replies will be sent to the selected recipient.

More Options!

You can configure your e-mail account to have all replies sent to another address. In Outlook, click Tools and then Account Settings. Click the E-mail tab, click the account with which you want to work, and then click Change. In the Change E-mail Account dialog box, click More Settings. In the Internet E-mail Settings dialog box, click the General tab and then type the reply address in the Reply E-mail text box. Click OK, click Next, click Finish, and then click Close.

Customize a Personal Distribution List

You can use a personal distribution list to send e-mail messages to a select group of people from your Outlook Address Book.

A distribution list can really help you speed up the task of e-mailing several people with the same message. You can also add and remove names from a personal distribution list.

Outlook marks distribution lists with a special icon that shows several faces. Outlook stores all distribution lists you create in the default Contacts folder. This feature allows you to quickly and easily assign categories to the lists as needed.

---

① Click File.

② Click New.

③ Click Distribution List.

Note: *You can also run the Distribution List command by pressing Ctrl+Shift+L.*

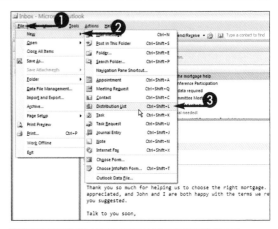

The Distribution List window appears.

④ Type a name for the list.

⑤ Click Select Members.

● To add members who are not in your Contacts list, you can click Add New.

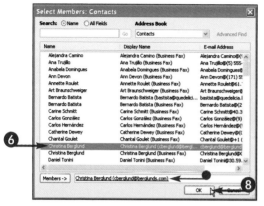

The Select Members dialog box opens.

⑥ Double-click the name you want to add.

● Outlook adds the contact to the distribution list.

⑦ Repeat Step **6** to continue adding names to the list.

⑧ Click OK.

● The distribution list shows the selected names.

⑨ Click Save & Close.

Office adds the list to your Address Book of e-mail addresses.

Apply It!

To use a distribution list in an e-mail message, click To in the message window, double-click the distribution list, and then click OK. Alternatively, open the Contacts folder, double-click the distribution list to open it, and then click E-mail. When you compose and send the message, Outlook sends it to everyone on the list.

Create a Custom Signature

You can add a signature to the bottom of your e-mail messages to include additional information about yourself or your company. You can also use signatures to share a favorite quote. Signatures are simply personalized information or a picture that you add to the end of your message.

You can use signatures to convey a message, such as how to respond to your e-mail. For example, if you send out an electronic newsletter in your e-mail that includes the latest product news of your company, you can add a signature at the bottom of the message that tells people how to unsubscribe to the list.

① Click Tools.

② Click Options.

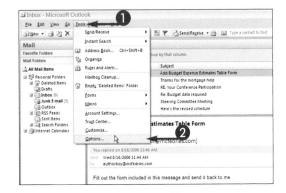

The Options dialog box appears.

③ Click the Mail Format tab.

④ Click Signatures.

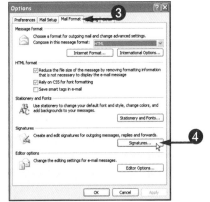

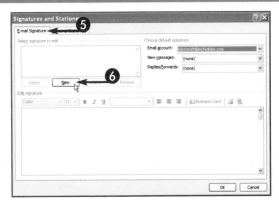

The Signatures and Stationery dialog box appears.

⑤ Click the E-mail Signature tab.

⑥ Click New.

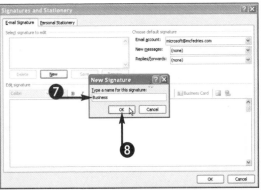

The New Signature dialog box appears.

⑦ Type a name for the signature.

⑧ Click OK.

Did You Know?

You can set up Outlook to add signatures automatically, as explained on the next page. However, you can also insert signatures by hand. Start a new message, and click the Message tab. In the Include group, click the Signature button to display a list of your signatures, and then click the signature you want to insert. Note, too, that you can also click the Signatures command to open the Signatures and Stationery dialog box.

continued

Create a Custom
Signature (continued)

When you create a new signature, you can indicate what formatting you want to use. You can also control the alignment of text in a signature or add bullets in front of the signature text.

You can save several signatures to use with different types of messages, as well as apply different signatures to new messages and to message replies and forwards.

You can also attach a virtual business card — sometimes called a *vCard* — to your signature. You can turn an Outlook contact into a vCard that you can share with other users. Attaching a vCard does not add the vCard text to your actual signature, but automatically attaches the information as a file attachment to the message.

---

⑨ Type your signature text.

● You can format the text.

● You can add a business card.

● You can add a picture.

⑩ Click OK.

⑪ Repeat Steps **6** to **10** to create other signatures.

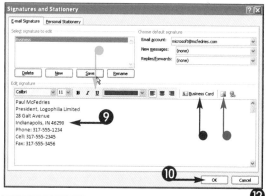

⑫ If you have multiple e-mail accounts, use the E-mail Account list to click the account to apply a signature to.

⑬ In the New Messages list, click the signature to add to new e-mail messages.

⑭ In the Replies/Forwards list, click the signature to add to replies and forwarded messages.

⑮ Click OK.

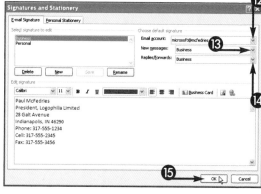

16 Click OK.

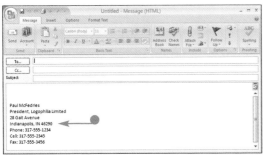

● Outlook applies the selected signature to any new messages you create.

Outlook also applies a signature to replies and forwarded messages if you selected an item in the Replies/Forwards list (Step **14**).

Try This!

To use the Business Card button, you must first create an item in the Contacts folder for yourself. Click Contacts, click New, and then type your name and other contact information. Click Save & Close. In the E-mail Signature tab, click the signature with which you want to work and then click Business Card. In the Insert Business Card dialog box, click your name and then click OK.

Clean a Mailbox of Space-Stealing Files

The more e-mail you receive through Outlook, the larger your Outlook mailbox becomes. If you use Outlook on a network, you may need to clean out your mailbox from time to time if it exceeds the size limits that your network allows. Cleaning out your mailbox regularly even if you do not use Outlook in a corporate network environment is a good idea. As messages pile up in your mailbox, they consume space on your computer as well.

If you worry about removing important messages, you can create a customized search to locate only the messages consuming the most space, such as those with file attachments.

① Click Tools.

② Click Instant Search.

③ Click Advanced Find.

You can also press Ctrl+Shift+F.

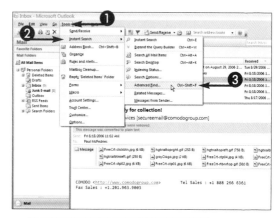

The Advanced Find dialog box appears.

④ Make sure you select Messages in the Look For box.

⑤ Click the More Choices tab.

⑥ Use the Size list to click Greater Than.

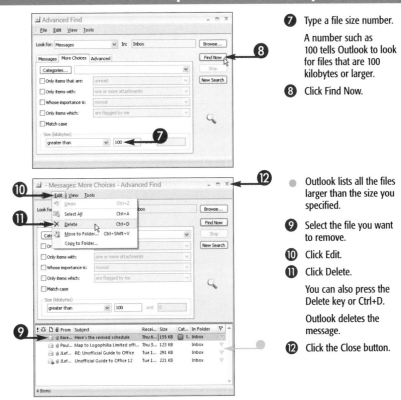

⑦ Type a file size number.

A number such as 100 tells Outlook to look for files that are 100 kilobytes or larger.

⑧ Click Find Now.

● Outlook lists all the files larger than the size you specified.

⑨ Select the file you want to remove.

⑩ Click Edit.

⑪ Click Delete.

You can also press the Delete key or Ctrl+D.

Outlook deletes the message.

⑫ Click the Close button.

Apply It!

To save a search you want to use again, click File, and then click Save Search to open the Save Search dialog box. Type a distinct name for the search and click OK. To reuse the search, open the Advanced Find dialog box, click File, click Open Search, and select the search.

Storing all of your contact names and addresses, including e-mail addresses, electronically can cause concern, especially if you worry about losing your data during a system crash.

The Outlook Address Book window does not offer a print option. However, you can print your contacts from the Contacts

folder. The Outlook Contacts folder enables you to record information about people you contact, such as family members, business contacts, and colleagues. In addition, it includes your e-mail address book.

The Print dialog box offers several different print styles.

---

① Click Contacts.

② Click File.

③ Click Print.

The Print dialog box appears.

④ Scroll through the Print Style list and click a style you want to use.

● If you want to see what your printout will look like before printing, click Preview.

⑤ Click OK.

Outlook prints your contacts, including e-mail addresses.

You can use the Outlook Contacts folder to easily insert names and addresses on envelopes or labels. With help from the Word Envelopes and Labels feature, you can quickly print out any name and address from your Outlook Address Book. You can leave Outlook open while you switch over to the Word window to access the Envelopes and Labels feature. The following steps focus on creating an envelope out of a contact using the Envelopes and Labels dialog box; however, you can also click the Labels tab and create a label just as easily.

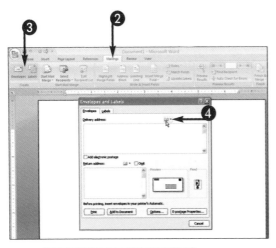

① With Outlook still open, switch to the Word window.

② Click Mailings.

③ Click Envelopes or Labels.

The Envelopes and Labels dialog box opens.

④ Click the Insert Address icon.

The Select Name dialog box opens.

⑤ Click the contact you want to use.

⑥ Click OK.

Outlook inserts the contact's address into the Delivery Address text box in the Envelopes and Labels dialog box.

You can now continue through the steps necessary to print an envelope in Word.

You can use your Internet connection to quickly find a map to the address of any contact in the Outlook Contacts folder.

This feature only works if you have an Internet connection. When you activate this feature, your default Web browser

window opens and connects you to the Windows Live Local Web site for looking up maps and addresses.

Using the Microsoft Virtual Earth technology, you can look up an address anywhere in the United States.

---

① Connect to the Internet.

② Double-click a contact in the Outlook Contacts list.

● The contact information appears.

● If the contact has more than one address, you can click the Addresses list and select an address to look up.

③ Click Contact.

④ Click Map.

Your default Web browser opens and displays a map to the address.

● You can using the Driving direction feature to get directions to the contact from an address you specify.

● You can use the Print feature to print out a copy of the map.

Although the Outlook Calendar view shows consecutive dates by default, you may need to see several nonconsecutive days side by side. For example, you can compare your schedule with similar dates in previous months, or view all the days that you met with the same client. Viewing nonconsecutive dates allows you to access associated meeting summaries, attachments, and meeting attendees. Outlook can display up to 14 nonconsecutive days in your calendar.

This technique works best in Day view; in Work Week or Week view, Outlook displays the selected nonconsecutive date alongside the displayed week.

① Click Calendar.

② Click Day.

③ Click the first date you want to view.

④ Press and hold the Ctrl key and click the next nonconsecutive date you want to view.

Note: *If you accidentally click the wrong date while pressing the Ctrl key, you can click the same date again to deselect it.*

● Outlook displays the new date next to the first date you selected.

Repeat Step **4** to select additional dates.

Note: *You can select up to 14 nonconsecutive dates to view in the calendar.*

Display Two Time Zones

You can tell Outlook to display two time zones in your calendar. This feature is particularly useful if your company works with offices across several states or around the globe.

When you add another time zone to your calendar, the hourly increments appear for both zones in the Day and Work Week calendar views. Adding another time zone to your calendar does not change the way your appointments and calendar notes appear. Office lists the hours for the extra time zone on the far left side of the calendar. You can also include a label for the newly added time zone so you can easily determine which zone is which. You can use a default label that describes the time zone, or you can create your own unique label for the zone.

① **Right-click the time grid.**

② **Click Change Time Zone.**

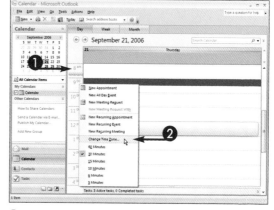

● The Time Zone dialog box appears.

③ Use this Label text box to type a brief label for the current time zone.

④ Click the Show an Additional Time Zone check box (☐ changes to ☑).

⑤ Use this Label text box to type a brief label for the new time zone.

⑥ Use the Time Zone list to click the time zone you want to include.

7 Click OK.

● Outlook displays two time zones in your calendar.

More Options!
By default, Outlook displays the original time zone on the right and the new time zone on the left. To switch the time zone positions, right-click the time grid and then click Change Time Zone to return to the Time Zone dialog box. Click Swap Time Zones and then click OK.

Chapter 6

Improve Your Database Productivity Using Access

Of all the Microsoft Office programs, Access has a reputation for being the most challenging application to use. After all, building and maintaining a database is not a simple task. Access is a complex and powerful tool that allows you to organize and track many types of data. Because of the complexity of the application, the makers of Access have included wizards to help users build individual components of a database. You should take advantage of these wizards: They can reduce the time you would spend to build database objects on your own.

Whether you are creating a database to track your DVDs, or a database to track

purchases for a corporation, this chapter offers unique techniques to make Access easier and more fun to use. For example, you can learn how to create your own splash screen, open specific records automatically, add visual interest to forms by adding background pictures, and more. When it comes to customizing your database objects – tables, queries, forms, and reports – Design view is the way to go. With Design view, you can quickly access various tools for controlling how an object looks and behaves. With the help of the tasks in this chapter, you can find a few new ways to become more productive without needing to become a database professional.

Quick Tips

You can create a custom splash screen that appears every time you open your Access database. Splash screens appear for just a moment as the database file opens. By default, an Access splash screen appears when you start Access. The default splash screen displays the name of the program, the version number, product ID number, and copyright information. You can create a custom splash screen that includes your name, your company name and logo, or a slogan. You can use a graphic file saved in the bitmap file format to create your own splash screen.

To see the custom splash screen, you must open the database file directly from the My Computer or My Documents folder (or the Computer or Documents folder, in Windows Vista), or from the desktop.

① Open the Save As dialog box in the program you used to create the splash screen image.

This example uses the Windows Paint program.

② Assign the bitmap object the same name, and to the same location, as the Access database file.

Note: Make sure you store the image and the database file in the My Documents folder (or the Documents folder, in Windows Vista).

③ Click Save.

④ Click Close.

⑤ Click Start.

⑥ Click My Documents.

If you are using Windows Vista, click Documents, instead.

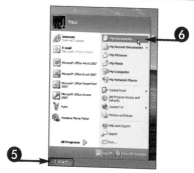

The My Documents window appears (or the Documents folder, in Windows Vista).

7. Double-click the database filename.

The Access program window opens and briefly displays your custom splash screen.

TIP

Important!

You must save the database file and the image in My Documents because that is a *trusted location* in Access 2007. If you use any other location, Access will not display the splash screen. To designate a folder as a trusted location, click Office, Access Options, Trust Center, and then Trust Center Settings. In the Trust Center, click Trusted Locations, Add New Location, specify the folder you want to use, and then click OK.

You can customize your database to display your own title in the title bar and your own icon in the taskbar.

By default, when you open a database file Access displays the database filename in the title bar and the regular Access icon in the taskbar button. Rather than sticking with these defaults, you can customize

both the title and icon. When you specify a custom title, Access displays the title in the title bar as well as in the database's taskbar button. When you specify a custom icon, Access displays the icon in the database's taskbar button. For the icon, you can either use an icon (.ico) file, if you have one, or a bitmap (.bmp) file.

① Open the database you want to customize.

② Click Office.

③ Click Access Options.

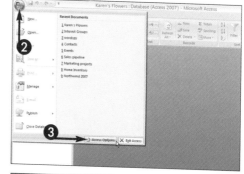

The Access Options dialog box appears.

④ Click Current Database.

⑤ Use the Application Title text box to type the database title you want to use.

⑥ Click Browse.

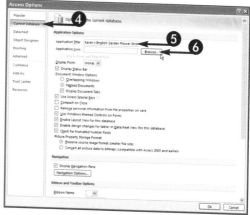

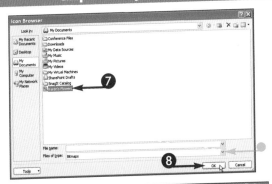

The Icon Browser dialog box appears.

● If you want to use a bitmap file, use the Files of Type list to click Bitmaps.

7 Click the image you want to use.

8 Click OK to close the Icon Browser dialog box.

9 Click OK to close the Access Options dialog box.

● Access applies the title to the title bar and taskbar button.

● Access applies the icon to the taskbar button.

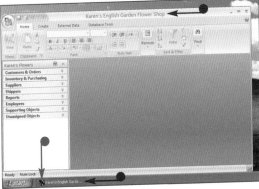

TIP

More Options!
You can also use the icon you applied to the database file as the icon that Access uses for forms and report. Follow Steps **1** to **8** to select an icon, if you have not done so already. With the Access Options dialog box still open, click the Use as Form and Report Icon check box (☐ changes to ☑). Click OK. Now, when you open a form or report, Access displays the icon in the form or report's tab.

Make a Database Window Work Like a Web Browser

By default, the Database window in Access works like an Explorer window. Objects appear as icons in the Navigation pane, and to open an object you double-click it. You can make your Navigation pane work more like a Web browser by changing the way in which the objects appear. Rather than viewing objects as icons, you can turn them into links that, when clicked, open the object. You may find this environment faster and more intuitive to work with if you frequently use both your Web browser and your Access databases.

① Right-click the Navigation pane header.

② Click Navigation Options.

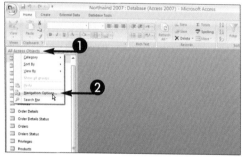

The Navigation Options dialog box appears.

③ Click the Single-click option (○ changes to ◉).

④ Click OK.

Database window objects now operate as links.

● Move your mouse pointer over an object to select it, and click to open it.

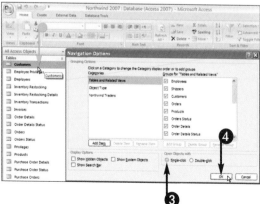

Databases often contain vast amounts of data, but to display all the data, the entry fields are often small and limited in space. You can edit your entries directly; however, you often cannot see the entire entry, or the text size for the entry appears too small to view comfortably.

You can use the Zoom dialog box to increase the magnification of an entry to more easily view and edit your field, text box, or property settings. After you make your edits and close the dialog box, the changes to the field, text box, or property setting immediately take effect.

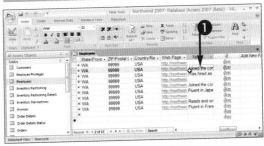

① Click in the field, text box, or property setting you want to view.

② Press Shift+F2.

The Zoom dialog box appears.

③ Make any edits you want to the entry.

● To change the font to a more legible size, click the Font button to open the Font dialog box and change the settings.

④ Click OK.

The Zoom dialog box closes.

Make Form Values Stand Out with Conditional Formatting

You can make certain form values stand out from the other values by applying a different type of formatting to those values.

When you view each record using your form, most of the time the data is easiest to read when you use the same font for every field. However, instances may occur where you want certain anomalous values to stand out from the others. For

example, in the Order List form in the sample Northwind database, you might want to display the Order Total value in a different color if that value is greater than $1,000.

Access forms support a feature called *conditional formatting* that enables you to apply a particular font automatically when a control value meets a specified condition.

① In the Navigation tab, right-click the form with which you want to work.

② Click Design View.

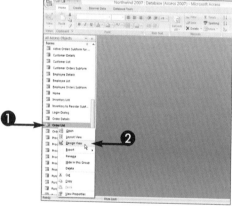

Access displays the form in Design view.

③ Click the field with which you want to work.

④ Click Design.

⑤ Click Conditional.

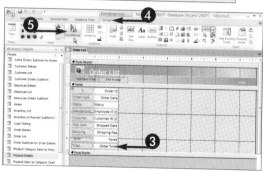

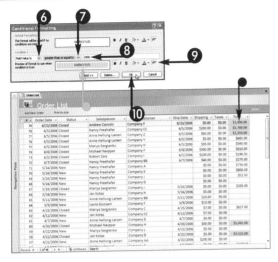

The Conditional Formatting dialog box appears.

6 Use the first Condition list to click Field Value Is.

7 Use the second Condition list to click the operator you want to use.

8 Use the Condition text box to type a value.

9 Use these controls to specify the format you want Access to use for values that match the Condition.

● This area shows you a preview of the format.

10 Click OK.

● Access applies the formatting to values that match the condition.

Did You Know?

Using the first Condition list, you can set up three different types of condition. If you click Field Value Is, the condition is applied to the current value of the field. In this case, you construct the condition by clicking a comparison operator (such as Between or Less Than) in the second list, and then typing one or two values (depending on the operator). If you click Expression Is, the condition is met when the logical expression you specify returns True. For example, if you type Date()=#8/23/2007#, the formatting is applied only on August 23, 2007. If you click Field Has Focus, the condition is met when the user moves the cursor into the field.

When you open a database, you can configure Access to automatically display the form you use most often.

If you frequently work with the same database in Access, you may have a particular form that you use first or that

you leave open while you work with the database. You can save yourself a few steps by configuring the database to always display that form each time you open the database.

① Click Office.

② Click Access Options.

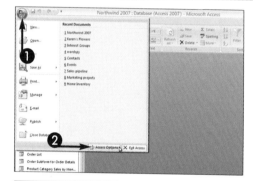

The Access Options dialog box appears.

③ Click Current Database.

④ Use the Display Form list to click the name of the form you want to open.

⑤ Click OK.

The next time you open the database file, the form you specify opens automatically.

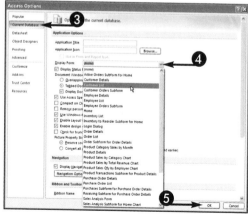

Most users press the Tab key to move from one field to the next in an Access form. You can control the direction in which the Tab key takes the user by specifying a *tab order*. By default, Access sets the tab order from left to right and from top to bottom.

To change the tab order, you must view the form in Design view. You can use the Tab Order dialog box to reorder the fields for tabbing. To return a custom tab order back into the left-to-right and top-to-bottom order, you can click the Auto Order button.

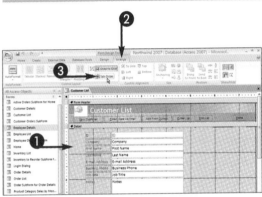

① Open the form in Design view.

Note: *Right-click any object and then click Design View to open the object in Design view.*

② Click Arrange.

③ Click Tab Order.

The Tab Order dialog box appears.

● Use this column to select and drag fields.

④ In the Custom Order list, select the field you want to move.

⑤ Drag the field up or down in the list and then drop it in the position you want.

⑥ Repeat Steps **4** and **5** to reorder any other fields you want.

⑦ Click OK.

Access assigns the new tab order to the form.

Make a Form Interesting by Adding a Picture

Forms offer an easy way to enter data into your table, but they are not very interesting on their own. If other people use your database, you may want to add an image or graphic to make your form more visually appealing.

You can add pictures to your Access forms using Design view. Design view lets you

resize the form to accommodate a picture or graphic object. Using the Image tool, you can determine the size and the placement of the image that you want to appear on the form. After defining the picture parameters, you can select the file you want to insert.

---

① Open the form to which you want to add a graphic in Design view.

Note: *Right-click any object and then click Design View to open the object in Design view.*

② Click and drag a corner or edge of the form to make room for the graphic object.

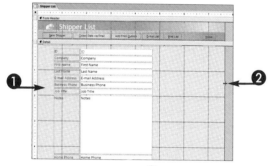

③ Click Design.

④ Click the Image button.

⑤ Click and drag on the form to create a placeholder for the graphic object.

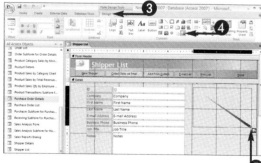

The Insert Picture dialog box appears.

6 Click the image file you want to insert.

7 Click OK.

Note: If you are adding a picture to a data access page, you click Insert instead of OK.

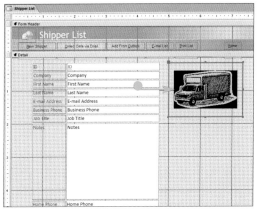

● The image appears on the form.

When you switch to Form view, you may need to resize the Form window to see the image that you add.

Did You Know?

You can apply formatting to an image object. In Design view, right-click the image. A shortcut menu appears with formatting controls, including commands for changing the fill or background color, and adding a stylized effect. For more image-formatting options, you can open the image's properties sheet, or you can open the Properties dialog box by right-clicking the image and then clicking Properties.

You can instruct Access to open a specific record in a form automatically when you open the form. By default, Access displays the first record in the underlying record set when you open a form.

You can use the GoToRecord VBA method in the form's Open event to open a specific record the next time you open the form.

To use this technique, you must type some code in the control object's On Open event. You can enter VBA code using the Code Builder window. When entering the code, you must substitute the name of your own form and make sure you know which record number you want to display automatically.

---

① Open the form you want to edit in Design view.

Note: *Right-click any object and then click Design View to open the object in Design view.*

② Click Design.

③ Click Property Sheet.

● You can also double-click the selector box for the form.

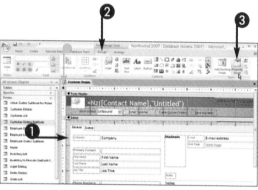

The Property Sheet pane appears.

④ Use the Selection Type list to click Form.

⑤ Click the Event tab.

⑥ Click the On Open event field.

⑦ Click the Build button.

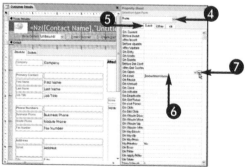

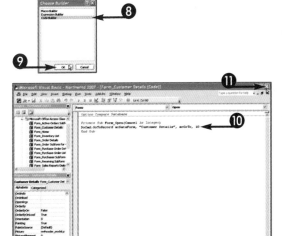

The Choose Builder dialog box appears.

8 Click Code Builder.

9 Click OK.

The Visual Basic window appears.

10 Type the code `DoCmd.GoToRecord acDataForm, "form", acGoTo, #`, replacing *form* with your own form name, and # with the number of the record you want to display.

11 Click the Visual Basic window's Close button.

12 Close the form and save your changes.

You can now test your code by reopening the form in Form view.

More Options!

Besides displaying a specific record number when you open a form, Access gives two other useful options. One option is to always display the last record when you open a form, which in most cases enables you to see the most recently added record. For this option replace `acGoTo, #` with `acLast`. The other option is to start a new record when you open the form, which is useful if you always open the form for data entry. In this case, replace `acGoTo, #` with `acNewRec`.

Set Up Forms to Close Automatically

You can have a frequently used form automatically close after a specific amount of time. To set an automatic close, switch to the Design view mode for your form and make changes to the form's properties sheet. You set a time interval using the Timer Interval property in the form's properties. The value is measured in thousandths of a second, so an entry of 3,000 equals 3 seconds.

After establishing a time value, you must add a string of VBA code into the On Timer property, using the Visual Basic code window. After adding the code string, you can return to the form's Design view and save the form.

---

① Open the form in Design view.

Note: Right-click any object and then click Design View to open the object in Design view.

② Click Design.

③ Click Property Sheet.

● You can also double-click the selector box for the form.

The Property Sheet pane appears.

④ Use the Selection Type list to click Form.

⑤ Click the Event tab.

⑥ Scroll down the property list and click Timer Interval property.

⑦ Set the number of seconds you want to leave the form open.

In this example, the value 60000 leaves the form open for 60 seconds.

⑧ Click the On Timer property.

⑨ Click the Builder button.

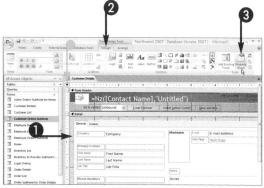

178

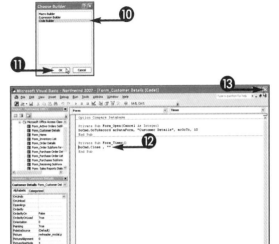

The Choose Builder dialog box appears.

⑩ Click Code Builder.

⑪ Click OK.

The Visual Basic window appears.

⑫ Type
DoCmd.Close,"".

⑬ Click the Visual Basic window's Close button.

⑭ Close the form and save your changes.

You can reopen the form in Form view to test the timer.

Remove It!

To remove a timer interval you assign to a form, follow Steps **1** to **5** to reopen the form in Design view and display the form's Event tab. Click inside the On Timer property and delete the [Event Procedure] text. Click inside the Timer Interval property and change the value to 0.

You can force Access to display an ampersand character (&) in a caption label property of a control. Normally, when you type an ampersand in a label, Access assumes that the character following the ampersand is the control's accelerator key. For example, if the caption label is &Name, Access displays the label as Name, and you can press Alt+N to select the control.

However, sometimes you may want the ampersand to appear. For example, if you type the name **Electric Power & Light**, Access displays the name as Electric Power_Light. To remedy this problem, you must specify two ampersands in the label instead of one.

① Open the form you want to edit in Design view.

Note: *Right-click any object and then click Design View to open the object in Design view.*

② Click the label you want to edit.

③ Click inside the label at the point where you want to edit the label text.

④ Edit the label text to include two ampersand symbols instead of one.

⑤ Click anywhere outside the label box.

● Access displays a single ampersand in the caption label.

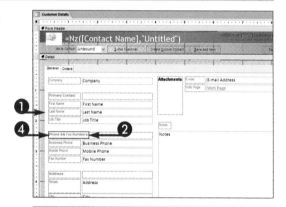

When you build a table in Access, you can have some field values display default values to make the table more convenient to use. You can specify a value that appears in the field by default, until the user changes it to another value. For example, perhaps you have an order-processing table that includes a field for specifying payment type. Payment type choices may include Credit Card, Check, or Cash. If the majority of the time the payment type is Credit Card, you can make Credit Card the default value that appears in the field automatically.

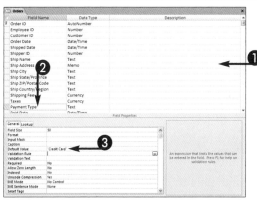

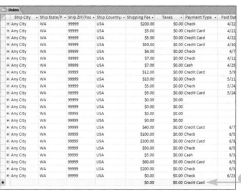

① Open the table in Design view.

Note: Right-click any object and then click Design View to open the object in Design view.

② Click the field you want to edit.

③ Type a default value in the Default Value property field.

Access applies the new value to any new records you create.

● When you save and close the table, Access applies the new default value to any new records you add in Datasheet view.

You can edit fields faster by configuring Access to automatically place the cursor at the end of each field as you enter the field.

When you use Tab or the arrow keys to navigate a datasheet, as you enter each field Access selects the entire field contents. If you do not want to replace the entire value, you must press F2 to place the cursor in the field. To avoid the extra step of pressing F2, you can configure Access to immediately place the cursor at the end of the field. Note that if you do this, then you must use Tab and Shift+Tab to navigate fields horizontally.

① Click Office.

② Click Access Options.

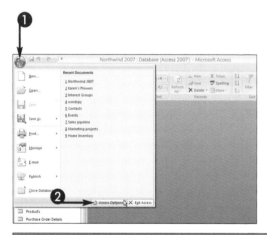

The Access Options dialog box appears.

③ Click Advanced.

④ Click Go to End of Field (○ changes to ◉).

● If you would prefer to always start at the beginning of each field, click Go to Start of Field (○ changes to ◉), instead.

⑤ Click OK.

When you navigate a datasheet with the keyboard, Access places the cursor at the end of each field automatically.

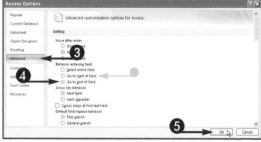

If you are repeatedly entering the same value in the same field in a table or form, you can use a shortcut technique to copy the value of the previous record. Rather than retype it, you can press a keyboard shortcut instead. This method can reduce the time you spend entering records into tables or forms.

To make the best use of this shortcut technique, you can type your record data in table form using Datasheet view. This view allows you to see the values that you typed into the same field for a previous record.

1 Open or start a blank record.

2 Click the field in which you want to copy a value.

3 Press Ctrl+'.

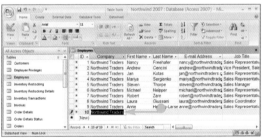

● Access immediately copies the value from the previous field.

Understanding the relationships between tables is an important part of building a successful database. Good database designers always evaluate the relationships between database tables.

Ordinarily, you can view table relationships using the Relationships window. To help you analyze the connections between

tables, you can print out a copy of the map of table relationships.

When you activate the Print Relationships command, Access automatically generates a report of the table relationships and switches you to Print Layout view. You can use this view mode to see the map layout and to activate the Print command.

1 Click Database Tools.

2 Click Relationships.

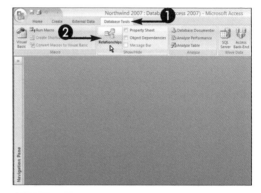

The Relationships window appears.

3 Click Design.

4 Click Relationship Report.

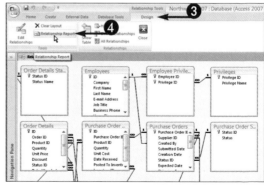

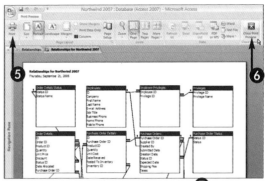

Access creates a report of the table relationships and opens the report in Print Preview mode.

⑤ Click Print.

⑥ Click Close Print Preview.

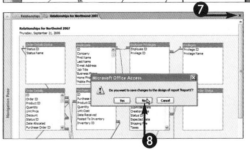

⑦ Click the Report window's Close button to close the report.

A prompt window appears, asking whether you want to save the report.

⑧ Click No to exit the report window without saving the report.

Did You Know?

If the relationships report looks jumbled when you view it in the Print Preview mode, you can rearrange the tables to make the report easier to read. Close the report and return to the Relationships window. Use your mouse to click and drag the tables into a layout that you prefer. When you are done, right-click an empty section of the window and then click Save Layout.

You can copy records from one table and append them to another table using the Navigation pane.

Ordinarily, you use an *append query* to copy certain records from one table and add them to the end of another table. However, if you want to append all of a table's records to another table, Access gives you an easier method: copy and paste within the Navigation pane. The

Paste Table As dialog box offers three choices for the data to copy. To append data, you type the name of the table to which you are appending data, and then activate the Append Data to Existing Table option. To paste the table structure without the table contents, you select the Structure Only option. To paste the structure and the data, you activate the Structure and Data option.

① Right-click the table that contains the records that you want to copy to another table.

② Click Copy.

③ Right-click anywhere in the Navigation pane.

④ Click Paste.

● The Paste Table As dialog box appears.

⑤ Type the name of the table to which you want to append data.

⑥ Click the Append Data to Existing Table option (○ changes to ◉).

⑦ Click OK.

Access appends the records.

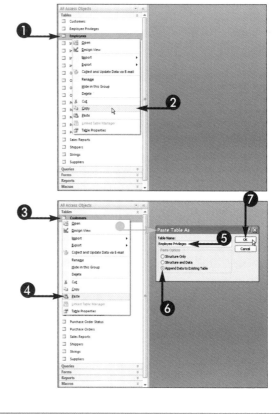

To keep your database file running efficiently, you can compact the database. Compacting is a periodic maintenance task that allows you to recover wasted disk space.

You can use the Compact feature to reclaim space left by deleted records and data. If you work every day with a database, compacting it at least once a week to keep the database file running efficiently is a good idea.

① Click Office.

② Click Access Options.

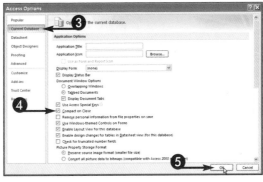

The Access Options dialog box appears.

③ Click Current Database.

④ Click the Compact on Close option (☐ changes to ☑).

⑤ Click OK.

When you close the file, Access compacts the database.

You can use input masks, also called field templates, to control how users enter data into a table field.

A common database problem is data entered inconsistently. For example, consider the following phone numbers: (123)555-6789, 123-555-6789, and 1235556789. These kinds of inconsistencies can cause all kinds of problems, from other users misreading the data, to improper sorting, to difficulties analyzing or querying the data.

A solution is to use an input mask, which is a kind of template that shows users how to enter the data. For example, here is an input mask for a phone number:

(___)___-____

Each underscore (_) acts as a placeholder for (in this case) a digit, and the parentheses and dash appear automatically as the user enters the number.

---

① Open the table in Design view.

Note: *Right-click any object and then click Design View to open the object in Design view.*

② Click the field you want to edit.

③ Click the Input Mask field property.

④ Click the Build button.

If the table has unsaved changes, Access prompts you to save the table.

⑤ Click Yes.

The Input Mask Wizard dialog box appears.

⑥ Click the Input Mask you want to assign.

● Click inside the Try It field if you want to test the data entry.

⑦ Click Next.

● If the predefined input mask is exactly what you need, click Finish, instead.

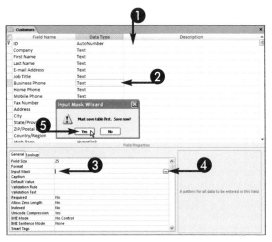

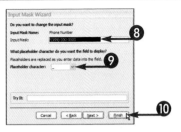

⑧ Adjust the Input Mask, as required.

⑨ Use the Placeholder Character list to click the character you want to use as a placeholder in the input mask.

⑩ Click Finish.

● Access assigns the Input Mask field property.

Any future values that you type must meet the criteria you define.

TIP

More Options!
When adjusting a predefined input mask, use the backslash character (\) to tell Access to display the following character as a literal; for example, \(is displayed as (. For placeholders, use 0 for a required digit or 9 for an optional digit; use L for a required letter or ? for an optional letter; use a for a required digit or letter or A for an optional digit or letter; use & for any required character or C for any optional character.

Force Page Breaks after Report Sections

You can configure a report to automatically begin a new page after a particular section.

You can often make a report more readable by starting a particular section (such as a grouping) on a new page. You do this by modifying a section's Force New Page property. This property has three possible values: Use the Before Section value to force a page break before the section to ensure that the section begins at the top of a new page; use the After Section value to force a page break after the section, which ensures that the next section begins at the top of a new page; use the Before & After value to force page breaks before and after the section, which ensures that the section appears on a page by itself.

① Open the report you want to work with in Design view.

Note: Right-click any object and then click Design View to open the object in Design view.

② Right-click an empty part of the section with which you want to work.

③ Click Properties.

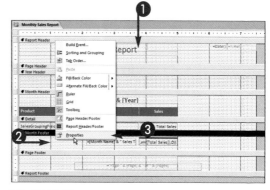

Access displays the Property Sheet pane.

④ Click the Format tab.

⑤ Use the Force New Page list to click the property value you want to use.

When you preview or print the report, Access forces page breaks according to the value selected.

You can make a report more readable by configuring it to avoid widowed controls and fields.

In a report, a *widow* is a control or field that appears at the top of a new page by itself when you preview or print the report. In most cases, the report will be more readable if you avoid widows and force all the elements of a section to appear together on the page. You can accomplish this task by activating the section's Keep Together property.

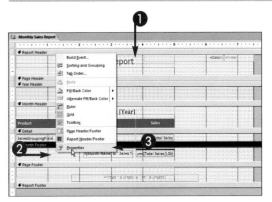

① Open the report you want to work with in Design view.

Note: *Right-click any object and then click Design View to open the object in Design view.*

② Right-click an empty part of the section with which you want to work.

③ Click Properties.

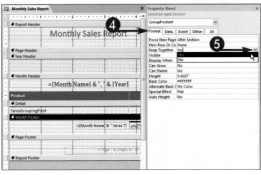

Access displays the Property Sheet pane.

④ Click the Format tab.

⑤ Use the Keep Together list to click Yes.

When you preview or print the report, Access keeps all the section's elements together on the page.

You can make tables, queries, and reports accessible to remote users by exporting the data to a Web page.

If you want another person to view a table, query, or report from a database, sending the database itself (via e-mail, for example) is not always convenient. The database might be quite large, or it might include sensitive data that you do not want the other user to see. Another problem is that the other person might not even have Access.

You can work around all of these problems by exporting the table, query, or report to a Web page. Access does this by creating a copy of the data using the HTML Document format, which is a format used by most Web pages.

① Select the table, query, or report you want to convert into a Web page.

② Click External Data.

③ Click More.

④ Click HTML Document.

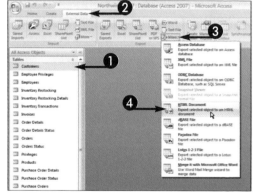

The Export - HTML Document dialog box appears.

⑤ Use the File Name text box to adjust the location and name of the Web page file.

⑥ Click Export Data with Formatting and Layout (☐ changes to ☑).

⑦ Click Open the Destination File After the Export Operation is Complete (☐ changes to ☑).

⑧ Click OK.

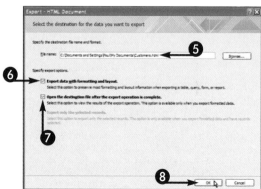

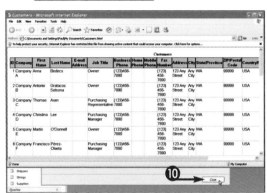

- The HTML Output Options dialog box appears.

9 Click OK.

Access displays the page in your Web browser.

10 Click Close in the Export - HTML Document dialog box.

More Options!

You can also export a table, query, or report to other file formats. For example, you can export data to an Excel spreadsheet file, a Rich Text Format (RTF) file that is compatible with Word, or to a text file. Follow Steps **1** and **2** and then click the format you want: Excel, Word, or Text File. You can also click More to see extra file formats such as dBASE, Paradox, and Lotus 1-2-3. In each case, you see a version of the Export dialog box, the layout of which depends on the file format you choose.

Office Shortcuts

General Office Shortcuts

Action	Shortcut Key
Cut	Ctrl+X
Copy	Ctrl+C
Paste	Ctrl+V
Open	Ctrl+O
Cycle between open windows	Alt+Tab
Close a document	Ctrl+W
Close the program window	Alt+F4
Save	Ctrl+S
Open the Save As dialog box	F12
New document	Ctrl+N
Print	Ctrl+P
Select All	Ctrl+A
Find	Ctrl+F
Replace	Ctrl+H
Go To	Ctrl+G
Toggle Ribbon on and off	Ctrl+F1
Help	F1
Spelling	F7
Undo	Ctrl+Z
Redo	Ctrl+Y
Bold	Ctrl+B
Italics	Ctrl+I
Underline	Ctrl+U
Subscript	Ctrl+=
Superscript	Ctrl+Shift++ (plus sign)
Cycle through upper-, lower-, and title case	Shift+F3
Insert a hyperlink	Ctrl+K
Copy a picture of the screen to the Clipboard	Print Screen
Move to the end of a text line	End
Move to the beginning of a text line	Home
Open the Visual Basic Editor	Alt+F11

Word Shortcuts

Action	Shortcut Key
Move to the beginning of the current word	Ctrl+Left arrow
Move to the beginning of the next word	Ctrl+Right arrow
Move to the beginning of a paragraph	Ctrl+Up arrow
Move to the beginning of the next paragraph	Ctrl+Down arrow
Move to the end of the window	Ctrl+Alt+Page Down
Move to the start of the window	Ctrl+Alt+Page Up
Move to the end of the document	Ctrl+End
Move to the start of the document	Ctrl+Home
Move the current paragraph down by one paragraph	Alt+Shift+Down arrow
Move the current paragraph up by one paragraph	Alt+Shift+Up arrow
Delete from the current cursor position to the beginning of the word	Ctrl+Backspace
Delete from the current cursor position to the end of the word	Ctrl+Delete
Indent a paragraph	Ctrl+M
Remove an indent	Ctrl+Shift+M
Add a hanging indent	Ctrl+T
Remove a hanging indent	Ctrl+Shift+T
Center a paragraph	Ctrl+E
Left-align a paragraph	Ctrl+L
Right-align a paragraph	Ctrl+R
Justify a paragraph	Ctrl+J
Double underline	Ctrl+Shift+D
Underline each word	Ctrl+Shift+W
Create a non-breaking space	Ctrl+Shift+Spacebar
Create a page break	Ctrl+Enter
Create a line break	Shift+Enter
Remove all formatting	Ctrl+Shift+N
Insert the current date	Alt+Shift+D
Insert the current time	Alt+Shift+T
Set single-space line spacing	Ctrl+1
Set double-space line spacing	Ctrl+2
Set 1.5-line spacing	Ctrl+5

continued

Office Shortcuts

Action	Shortcut Key
Open the Macros dialog box	Alt+F8
Repeat previous search	Shift+F4
Cycle through last three edits	Shift+F5
Open the Thesaurus	Shift+F7
Repeat the most recent action	F4
Display Go To tab	F5
Open the Bookmark dialog box	Ctrl+Shift+F5
Activate the Select Browse Object button	Ctrl+Alt+Home
Navigate to the next Select Browse object	Ctrl+Page Down
Navigate to the previous Select Browse object	Ctrl+Page Up

Excel Shortcuts

Action	Shortcut Key
Edit cells	F2
Delete selected cells entirely	Ctrl+-
Move between open workbooks	Ctrl+Tab
Move to the next sheet	Ctrl+Page Down
Move to the previous sheet	Ctrl+Page Up
Insert a new worksheet	Shift+F11
Select the current sheet and the next sheet	Shift+Ctrl+Page Down
Select the current sheet and the previous sheet	Shift+Ctrl+Page Up
Select the entire column	Ctrl+Spacebar
Select the entire row	Shift+Spacebar
Display the Format Cells dialog box	Ctrl+1
Select a range of cells	Ctrl+Shift+*
Enter a line break within a cell	Alt+Enter
Toggle between absolute and relative cell references	F4
Toggle between viewing values and formulas in cells	Ctrl+`
Insert blank cells	Ctrl+Shift++
Hide the selected rows	Ctrl+9
Unhide any hidden rows in the selection	Ctrl+Shift+(
Hide the selected columns	Ctrl+0

Action	Shortcut Key
Unhide any hidden columns in the selection	Ctrl+Shift+)
Apply an outline border to the selected cells	Ctrl+Shift+&
Remove the outline border	Ctrl+Shift+_
Insert the current date	Ctrl+;
Insert the current time	Ctrl+Shift+;
Insert the current date and time	Ctrl+;+Spacebar and then Ctrl+Shift+;
Create a chart	F11
Repeat the last action	F4
Define a range name	Ctrl+F3
Fill a range to the right	Ctrl+R
Fill a range down	Ctrl+D
Enter the cent character	Alt+0162 (numeric keypad)
Enter the pound sterling character	Alt+0163 (numeric keypad)
Enter the yen symbol	Alt+0165 (numeric keypad)
Enter the euro symbol	Alt+0128 (numeric keypad)
Display the Insert Function dialog box	Shift+F3
Copy the value from the cell above	Ctrl+Shift+"
Copy the formula from the cell above	Ctrl+'
Edit a cell comment	Shift+F2
Apply the currency format	Ctrl+Shift+$
Apply the percentage format	Ctrl+Shift+%
Apply the exponential number format	Ctrl+Shift+^
Apply the number format with two decimals	Ctrl+Shift+!
Apply the general number format	Ctrl+Shift+~
Display the Style dialog box	Alt+'

PowerPoint Shortcuts

Action	Shortcut Key
Switch between Outline and Slide view	Ctrl+Shift+Tab
Insert a new slide	Ctrl+M
Duplicate the current slide	Ctrl+D
Increase font size	Ctrl+Shift+>
Decrease font size	Ctrl+Shift+<
Display the Font dialog box	Ctrl+T

continued

PowerPoint Shortcuts (continued)

Action	Shortcut Key
Open the properties for an object	Double-click the object
Promote a paragraph in an outline	Alt+Shift+Left arrow
Demote a paragraph in an outline	Alt+Shift+Right arrow
Move selected outline paragraphs up	Alt+Shift+Up arrow
Move selected outline paragraphs down	Alt+Shift+Down arrow
Display outline heading level 1	Alt+Shift+1
Expand outline text below a heading	Alt+Shift++
Collapse outline text below a heading	Alt+Shift+-
Collapse or show all text or headings	Alt+Shift+A
Show or hide the grid	Shift+F9
Show or hide guides	Alt+F9
Change grid and guide settings	Ctrl+G
Run a slide show	F5
Activate the Pen tool during a show	Ctrl+P
Erase Pen tool drawings during a show	E
Turn off the Pen tool	Esc
Change the pen to a pointer	Ctrl+A
Hide the pointer or pen	Ctrl+H
Move to the next hyperlink	Tab
Make the screen go black during a show	B
Make the screen go white during a show	W
Stop or restart an automatic show	S
Return to the first slide	1+Enter

Outlook Shortcuts

Action	Shortcut Key
Switch to Mail	Ctrl+1
Switch to Calendar	Ctrl+2
Switch to Contacts	Ctrl+3
Switch to Tasks	Ctrl+4
Switch to Notes	Ctrl+5
Switch to Folder List in the Navigation pane	Ctrl+6

Action	*Shortcut Key*
Switch to Shortcuts	Ctrl+7
Switch to Journal	Ctrl+8
Next message	Ctrl+,
Previous message	Ctrl+.
Create a new appointment	Ctrl+Shift+A
Create a new meeting request	Ctrl+Shift+Q
Create a new contact	Ctrl+Shift+C
Create a new distribution list	Ctrl+Shift+L
Create a new journal entry	Ctrl+Shift+J
Create a new task	Ctrl+Shift+K
Create a new task request	Ctrl+Shift+U
Create a new note	Ctrl+Shift+N
Create a new fax	Ctrl+Shift+X
Create a new e-mail message	Ctrl+Shift+M
Select the Inbox folder	Ctrl+Shift+I
Select the Outbox folder	Ctrl+Shift+O
Flag a message for follow-up	Ctrl+Shift+G
Forward a message	Ctrl+F
Send a message	Ctrl+Enter
Reply to a message	Ctrl+R
Reply All to a message	Ctrl+Shift+R
Check for new e-mail	Ctrl+M or F9
Open a received message	Ctrl+O
Mark a message as read	Ctrl+Q
Mark a message as unread	Ctrl+U
Create a new folder	Ctrl+Shift+E
Switch Calendar to Day view	Ctrl+Alt+1
Switch Calendar to Work Week view	Ctrl+Alt+2
Switch Calendar to Week view	Ctrl+Alt+3
Switch Calendar to Month view	Ctrl+Alt+4
Change the number of Calendar days that display	Alt+(any number from 1–10)
Go to a specific data in Calendar	Ctrl+G
Dial a contact phone number	Ctrl+Shift+D

Access Shortcuts

Action	Shortcut Key
Select the current column containing the selected cell in Datasheet view	Ctrl+Spacebar
Select the column to the right of the current column	Shift+Right arrow
Select the column to the left of the current column	Shift+Left arrow
Undo changes for the current field	Press Esc once
Undo changes for the current record	Press Esc twice
Insert the current date	Ctrl+;
Insert the current time	Ctrl+Shift+;
Insert the current date and time	Ctrl+;+Spacebar and then Ctrl+Shift+;
Insert the default field value	Ctrl+Alt+Spacebar
Insert the value of the previous record	Ctrl+'
Add a new record	Ctrl++
Delete the current record	Ctrl+–
Save changes to the current record	Shift+Enter
Requery	Shift+F9
Open a combo box	Alt+Down arrow
Display the property sheet in Design view	F4
Switch to Form view from Design view	F5
View or add code in Design view	F7
Switch between upper and lower window portions	F6
Cycle between open windows	Ctrl+F6
Open the Zoom box	Shift+F2
Rename a selected object in the Navigation pane	F2

Index

Symbols

& (ampersand)
  concatenation operator, 111
  as literal character, 180
\ (backslash), literal escape character, 189

A

absolute cell references, 89
Access databases
  & (ampersand), as literal character, 180
  Access Options dialog box, 166–167
  append queries, 186
  appending records, 186
  browser-like navigation, 168
  Code Builder window, 176–177
  compacting, 187
  copying previous record, 183
  default table values, 181
  exporting to Web pages, 192–193
  icon, customizing, 166–167
  jump to end of file, 182
  Paste Table As dialog box, 186
  performance optimization, 187
  Print Relationships command, 184–185
  Properties dialog box, 175
  Relationship window, 184–185
  save location, 165
  shortcut keys, 200
  splash screen, customizing, 164–165
  table relationship maps, 184–185
  titles, customizing, 166–167
  trusted locations, 165
  VBA code, 176–177
  Zoom dialog box, 169
  zooming in/out, 169
Access databases, printing
  Force New Page property, 190
  Keep Together property, 191
  page breaks, 190
  report readability, 185
  widows, 191
Access forms
  \ (backslash), literal escape character, 189
  always display last-used record, 177
  closing automatically, 178–179

conditional formatting, 170–171
  controlling user input, 188–189
  field templates, 188–189
  formatting objects, 174–175
  GoToRecord method, 176–177
  inconsistent data entry, 188–189
  input masks, 188–189
  new record on opening, 177
  opening records automatically, 176–177
  pictures, 174–175
  startup default, 172
  tab order, 173
  Tab Order dialog box, 173
  timer interval, 178–179
  Timer Interval property, 178–179
Address Book window, 156
address books, printing, 156. See also contacts;
Outlook.
addressing envelopes, 157
Advanced Find dialog box, 155
aligning objects
  documents, 71
  slides, 123
ampersand (&)
  concatenation operator, 111
  as literal character, 180
annotations
  removing from documents, 20–21
  scanned documents, 26–27
API for blog hosts, 39
append queries, 186
appending database records, 186
arrows, PowerPoint, 125
AutoRecover feature, 4–5
AutoText feature, 50–51

B

backgrounds
  removing, 31
  slides, 131
  worksheets, 99
backing up data. See AutoRecover feature.
backslash (\), literal escape character, 189
Block Arrows, PowerPoint, 125
Blog Post URL, 39

Index

continued

Index

Index

Index

continued

Index